Hidden in Plain Sight

A Story of Love and Loss

Brigitte Giglia

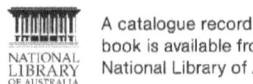 A catalogue record for this book is available from the National Library of Australia

Author Contact:
Mobile: 0407 382 995
Email: gigliabrigitte9@gmail.com
PO Box 7199
Safety Bay, WA 6169

First Edition
Printed in Australia

Copyright © 2025 Brigitte Giglia
All rights reserved.
ISBN-13: 978-1-923174-70-2

Linellen Press
265 Boomerang Road
Oldbury, Western Australia
Email: helen.iles.linpress@gmail.com

Dedication

Dave
You meant more to me than you ever knew.
I wish you'd seen yourself through my eyes.
I will always treasure the love we shared.
We were enough.

Joe
Thank you for giving me your name and a sense of security I never had before. We didn't always get it right, but there was love – and for that, I'll always be grateful.

For my children/grandchildren
No matter what my choices were, they were never a reflection of the love I hold for you.
You are my heart, my strength, and the reason I keep going.

This is a true story, told from memory and emotion. Some names or details have been changed to protect privacy, but the experiences are real and lived.

Contents

Dedication iii

Contents v

Introduction 3

Chapter 1 - Growing Into Myself 5

Chapter 2 - Joe: The Man 20

Chapter 3 - Dave 34

Chapter 4 - Lines Crossed 41

Chapter 5 - Finding Our Rhythm 52

Chapter 6 - The Gamble of Life 60

Chapter 7 - Addiction 65

Chapter 8 - Affairs of the Heart 76

Chapter 9 - A Christmas of Too Much 84

Chapter 10 - Birthday Love 89

Chapter 11 - Love Languages 94

Chapter 12 - Housesitting 102

Chapter 13 - My Favourite Italian 106

Chapter 14 - No Fuss, Just Us 116

Chapter 15 - An Isolated Incident 121

Chapter 16 - The Gardener 127

Chapter 17 - The Catch 134

Chapter 18 - Culinary Culture 140

Chapter 19 - Van Life 155

Chapter 20 - Working Through It 163

Chapter 21 - One for the Bucket List 170

Chapter 22 - Keeping Face 179

Chapter 23 - Fighting for Air 186

Chapter 24 - The Day the Music Died 197

Chapter 25 - Two Graves, One Heart 204

Chapter 26 - Turn the Volume Up 208

Chapter 27 - My Cup of Tea 215

Chapter 28 - The First Anniversary 217

Chapter 29 - It's Not Just a Hanky 220

Chapter 30 - Grief – Not So Quiet After all 223

Chapter 31 - The Anger of Grief 226

Chapter 32 - Let's Rock One Last Time 229

Chapter 33 - Final Word 231

About the Author 234

"'Tis better to have loved and lost
than never to have loved at all"

Alfred Lord Tennyson

Introduction

I'm not a celebrity. You won't find my name in the news or splashed across social media. I'm just an ordinary woman, like the neighbour you wave to, or the friend you share coffee with. But behind every ordinary woman is an extraordinary story. Mine is shaped by love, loss, and survival.

I never imagined I'd write a book. Grief and love taught me it's possible to honour the past while still embracing the future. These twin forces, so personal yet so universal, have carried me through a journey marked by hidden love and profound loss.

I loved two men in my lifetime, each in very different ways.

Joe, the man I married and the father of my children, taught me about responsibility and resilience. Our shared life shaped my understanding of marriage in all its complexity.

Then there was Dave, who came later and made me feel safe, seen, and whole. Our love was private, but no less real. It felt genuine and profound. When I think of Dave, I remember the safety of his arms, the quiet gestures of care, and how he gave me the courage to not be brave all the time.

Losing Joe was the first significant loss of my life. It broke my heart. Still, I was surrounded by family and friends, cushioned in grief, even as I struggled to understand a sorrow I'd never known.

Losing Dave was different, quieter, lonelier, more complex. It cut deeper and settled into my bones. But I've also learned that healing can live alongside it.

For too long, Dave and I worried about what other people thought, neighbours, coworkers, strangers who barely knew us.

I'm done worrying now. This is our story, told in my voice. Others might have seen glimpses from the outside, but only we knew the truth of what we lived.

Towards the end, when Dave was sick, all we wanted was peace. We saw clearly who showed love, and who didn't. That clarity changed everything.

This memoir isn't just a tribute to love or a goodbye to the men I've lost. It's a testament to endurance, truth, and the quiet power of telling your story on your own terms.

If you're reading this and you're struggling with grief, addiction, mental health, or just the weight of everyday life, please know you're not alone. There's no shame in needing help. Sometimes, simply naming your pain is its own kind of strength.

Chapter 1

Growing Into Myself

Growing up, I was the middle child, with an older sister and a younger brother. I was a skinny kid with unruly, wavy black hair. I'd run wild through the underdeveloped green pastures at the top of our street, chasing cows, getting zapped by electric fences, the cool wind on my face, barefoot and carefree. My toes were always stubbed, my knees always skinned. I was a tomboy.

My brother David, my older sister Leslie and me in the middle. Napier, New Zealand 1973

My father was an Englishman, born in Manchester, and my mother was a strong Māori woman who grew up in Tūrangi, New Zealand. Together, they were a mixed-race couple in the early 1960s, when prejudice still lingered. Growing up, we were the only family of mixed heritage on our street. When Mum left and Dad raised the three of us alone, he became a single father doing his best in a world still learning that it was okay to be different, regardless of the circumstances.

My parents divorced when I was eight, and I became a people pleaser. I felt that if I could keep the peace, everything would be fine. I became a caretaker of other people's problems far too young, and it taught me habits that set the tone for life.

Life with Dad as a single dad.
Sister Leslie on left, my brother David and I

I can't remember a childhood with two parents. But I remember the day a woman knocked on our door.

"Is your father home?" she asked.

When I said no, she looked straight at me and said, "When he gets home, tell him your mum has left with my husband."

What's a little kid supposed to do with that? I didn't understand it completely, but I knew she was mad.

Not long after, Dad started playing an old 45 on the record player. It was *It's All Over Now, Baby Blue* by Bob Dylan. I didn't know the song or who sang it back then, but I remember the look on Dad's face. I wasn't sad that Mum had gone, not then. I was sad because he was. That was all I could understand at that age.

Now, at fifty-nine, I realise that song I heard spinning over and over was Dylan. I still love his music. Maybe it started right there, with my dad sitting beside that record player, heartbroken.

When Dad heard where Mum might be, he said, "Which one of you kids is coming with me? Brigitte, you come."

My brother was too little, and my sister was too sensible. She would have talked him out of it before he got there. Me? I just went along for the ride, like I always did.

We ended up in a small town, Dad scanning the streets and shopfronts until he spotted her in a café. He sat me at the counter, facing the window, and walked away. I didn't know the plan. I just sat there, legs dangling, waiting.

When Mum came over to clear a table, she stopped in her tracks. "What are you doing here?" she said. She looked shocked, maybe nervous, her eyes flicking around the room to see where Dad was. I told her he'd left me there. She took me back with her to the hotel where she was staying.

Later, Dad showed up, and there was a confrontation. I don't remember feeling scared, but looking back, I can't imagine any child wouldn't have been.

A couple of days later, Mum put me on a plane back to Auckland. I suppose she had other plans then, ones that didn't include a child just yet. It was my first time on an aeroplane, and that's what I remember most - the small adventure of flying home. The rest, I've only unpacked as an adult.

Maybe that's why, even now, when I hear *It's All Over Now, Baby Blue*, I'm right back there: eight years old, legs swinging from a milk-bar stool, watching my dad's face as the record spins.

Though there was sadness, Dad still tried to bring happiness into our lives, and some memories still make me smile – like walking home from Little Athletics with him. The sky was deep and dark, scattered with stars. One of us would be perched high on his shoulders, soaking up his praises. Just before we reached the house, my brother and I would tear off down the street, racing the moon. Sometimes I'd grab his hand and urge him to run faster. He was such a quick little runner. He even made it into the paper once, holding a trophy almost bigger than him, grinning from ear to ear.

My sister walked behind us, calm and thoughtful. She was only about ten but had already stepped into a role of responsibility. While my brother and I were loud and full of energy, she was trying to keep our family together. She always looked after herself beautifully, even at that age – long, straight, shiny black hair and neat clothes. Somehow, she managed to stay composed while the rest of us were a shambles. My brother and I never cared what we looked like. She was different.

It's funny how the process of writing stirs up memories, some sweet, some sad. As a child, you don't always see the full picture. Now, with the eyes of an adult, I look back with a different kind of understanding. I see the quiet burden she carried, one I never noticed. We were still children, caught up in our childhood, while she had already stepped away from hers. What a loss that must have been. I see that now. That early split between childhood and responsibility stayed with us all, but in different ways.

Two years later, I remember Dad waving us off as we flew to Australia to live with Mum. I could see the sadness in his eyes. I didn't want him to feel that way, but I didn't know how to help. I felt a weight in my chest that wouldn't go away.

I was always Dad's girl. That never changed, even when I was grown. When he passed away ten years ago, I was heartbroken. But what cut deep was reading his will. Our names weren't in it – not mine, not my brother's, not my sister's. It was as if we didn't exist, as if we'd never been his children. I didn't care about getting anything; that wasn't what hurt. What hurt was being left out completely. Why do the people we love most have to disappoint us like that?

After the constant changes of those early years, our household eventually found its rhythm. We sat down for dinner together every night, and looking back, I realise how steadying that was. There wasn't drinking or partying in the house; Mum and my stepfather were adventurous instead. One Christmas holiday, we set off around Australia in a decked-out Land Cruiser, sailing in the Whitsundays and exploring the coast. Weekends were filled with four-wheel driving, canoe trips, and family outings to places like El Caballo Blanco or the Lion Park. At the time, I took it all for granted, but now I see how much effort went into giving us those memories.

Even then, I was still working out where I belonged, who I was in this new version of our family. Life at home settled into a pattern of its own. Home life had rules, too. Mum was strict, and bedtime was 8:30 even in high school. I didn't go out much, even though I was popular at school, and I often felt like I missed out socially.

It's hard to explain, but I didn't have the same kind of relationship with Mum that my friends had with theirs. Mum wasn't overly affectionate. She cared for us, made sure we were fed, clothed, and had what we needed, but hugs and heart-to-hearts weren't really her way. I can't remember big birthday parties or sleepovers in the lounge, but we still had a good life in our own way. Mum grew up without a mother herself. Her mum passed away when she was just a baby, and the nana who cared for her also died when she was still very young. So she never had that example of what motherly affection looked or felt like. As a child, I probably didn't question it; as a teenager, I started to notice; and now, as an adult, I see it with sadness, not blame, but empathy. She missed out on that kind of love, the kind only a mother can give, and in turn, so did we, though we didn't realise it at the time.

Still, when I look at the bigger picture, I can also see how strong my mum was. Against the odds, she built a whole new life in Australia. She held things together in her own way, and while I sometimes felt the gaps, I can't deny that her strength was undeniable. Whatever she faced, she carried on and made something for herself and for us.

I was also fortunate to have a stepfather who was a good man. I've heard horror stories from friends about theirs, and I thank God that wasn't my experience. He made things easier, and for that I'll always be grateful.

As a kid, I never thought much about identity or belonging. It's only later, when you start piecing together the odd little moments, that you realise how much they shaped who you became.

I remember one day when we were living in Australia, I must've been about ten, and Mum suddenly said to me, "You know, that's not how you spell your name."

I looked at her, confused. "What?"

I'd been spelling my name Bridget for as long as I could write. But now, out of nowhere, she tells me it's spelled Brigitte.

I didn't question it at the time. I just started spelling it differently. But later, I thought: how does that happen? Your name is something so important, it's your identity. It stays with you your whole life. Someone must have taught me to spell it that way; I wouldn't have just made it up, not as a kid. Even now, it still baffles me.

Then, when we moved to Newman in the Pilbara, I would've been about eleven. My mum decided to hyphenate our surname, and suddenly we were Theaker-Cook. Cook was my stepfather's surname, and I think maybe that was her way of making us look more like a proper family. Maybe it was about appearances, her insecurity, wanting to fit in, wanting people not to ask questions.

My older sister refused; she kept Theaker. My brother and I didn't think much about it when we were kids, and later, as adults, we just went along with it. Over time, the Theaker part was dropped altogether, and I just became Brigitte Cook.

That name stuck. When my daughter was born, I was listed on her birth certificate as Brigitte Cook, the name I'd been using for years.

It wasn't until I went to get my driver's licence that everything came undone. All my documents, school records, ID, and bank stuff were in Brigitte Cook. But legally, that wasn't my name. I didn't have a birth certificate to match any of it.

That's when I realised: this isn't who I am on paper, and yet it was the only version of me I'd ever known. I had to sort through everything just to prove who I was and then go back and have my daughter's birth certificate amended to match. That felt strange too, like the mother listed on her original birth certificate wasn't someone who truly existed.

It made me think about how easy it is to lose track of who you are, even in official records. You start off trying to belong, to fit, and somewhere along the line, your real name gets lost.

That was my history, and I wanted it to continue correctly. I remember thinking: I can't wait to get married and just be someone's wife. Maybe then the whole name business would finally make sense.

When I married Joe and became Brigitte Giglia, it felt like the first time my name belonged to me. It gave me something I hadn't felt before, a sense of identity.

By my early teens, I'd started to push boundaries. We were living in Newman in the Pilbara, miles from anywhere, surrounded by red dirt and spinifex. I'd sneak out at night or run away just to hang out with friends, putting myself at risk. Eventually, after much frustration, I was sent to live with Dad in New Zealand.

There, I was mostly left to my own devices. Dad hadn't been a full-time parent for years, and he and his partner had their own lives. I started a new school, made friends, and learned to take care of myself. Dad was affectionate and could always tell a good story, but at fourteen, I was largely fending for myself.

Two years later, I was sent back to Australia to live with Mum. I'm not sure why; maybe it had just become too hard to have a teenage daughter around. I do know I missed my brother and sister. But deep down, I felt like whenever I got too much, no one really wanted me anymore.

Regrettably, as a parent, I have passed some of that hurt on. My older two children probably bore the brunt of my instability and rash decisions. There were times I put my own need for change or happiness before their sense of security. I've heard their pain, and I carry it with deep regret. I am truly sorry.

When I reached my later teenage years, an inner conflict began to surface. I became rebellious and ran away from home, more than once. I think I was desperate to feel loved. I thought attention meant affection, that sex meant love. I didn't know any different.

I hadn't even finished growing up when, at seventeen, I found out I was pregnant. By eighteen, I was holding my baby in my arms.

*Day out with Mum before she left to live in Australia.
Me hugging my brother David, sister Leslie on right.*

The father was dangerous and violent, beginning each day with abuse. The abuse didn't always come with a warning. Sometimes, it came out of nowhere.

I remember waking up to a sudden yank, my scalp burning as he dragged me from the bed by my hair. My body hit the cold floor, still tangled in the fog of sleep, while my mind scrambled to understand what was happening.

His voice, sharp and enraged, cut through the darkness.

"Where are my socks?"

The words barely registered, but the fury behind them did. My chest tightened. My heart pounded like it might burst. I couldn't breathe or think, only feel the pain of his grip and the crushing weight of his anger. I was paralysed by a mix of fear and helplessness. I wanted to scream, to fight back, but all I could do was endure.

I remember another day, in public, when a man stepped in to defend me.

It only enraged him more.

I ran.

A blur of streets and fear.

Heart pounding, breath short, I ducked into a dimly lit car park. My body shook so violently that my teeth chattered. I held my breath. Strained to listen. Waited for the footsteps I knew would come.

His voice snapped through the air, venomous as ever, calling my name.

Before I could run again, he found me, hands grabbing, dragging me to the car.

A blur of movement.

Then a crack as my face smashed into the steering wheel.

Pain exploded through my cheekbones. My eyes swelled fast, the skin tightening and throbbing. Panic rose in my throat, but I held it down.

I had to stay still. Stay quiet. Survive this now. Run later, when it was safe.

I hid the bruises from family and strangers. Wore sunglasses in shops. Avoided eye contact. Hoped no one looked too closely.

I told myself they wouldn't understand.

Or maybe I just didn't want to see the look on their faces.

But not from my closest friends.

They were always there, standing by me, supporting whatever choices I made.

Still, the fear was impossible to fully hide.

For those who've never lived it, it's hard to understand how a home can become a prison, or how love can twist itself into something terrifying. You might wonder why someone stays, or how fear roots itself so deeply that even choosing what to cook for dinner feels dangerous.

But when the place that's supposed to keep you safe becomes the one you dread most, your whole sense of self begins to crumble.

And the hardest part is knowing that what you're missing, safety, love, peace, is something everyone deserves.

For years, I flinched at sudden noises. My heart raced whenever someone moved too fast. I was always waiting, always bracing for the next time, because there was always a next time.

The abuse left deep emotional scars. It made me doubt my worth and question whether I deserved to feel safe. I didn't know how to cope. I thought becoming a mother would fix everything. That it would give me the purpose I was so desperate for.

But life isn't that simple.

The day my daughter was born, she was tiny and perfect, with a full head of thick, black hair. I felt this deep, indescribable love. I was young, and I could feel the weight of people's judgment.

Visitors came and went, talking to other patients, but I was sure they were whispering about me.

Maybe they weren't.

Maybe they just saw a girl who thought she was grown, but wasn't.

At that moment, I realised how young I was.

I felt alone, with no time to undo anything.

This was my world now. This was my life.

Although my partner sat beside me, I couldn't call him a father.

I haven't seen him in over thirty-five years, and the only time I ever want to hear his name is when someone tells me he's dead.

Maybe we're not meant to voice those thoughts out loud, but it's the truth.

I don't think of him often, although some triggers take me straight back.

When a domestic violence story flashes up on the news, I can feel it through the screen, the fear, the pain, the helplessness of those women.

It brings it all back.

And still, it feels unfair that both fathers of my other children are now gone, and that man, the one who caused the most pain, is still out there somewhere.

Sometimes I wonder if there's truth in that old saying, "Only the good die young." The ones who hurt you the most seem to live the longest.

I finally mustered the courage to leave and moved into a shared house with housemates who could protect me when my abuser tried to force his way in. It offered a small semblance of safety during a dangerous time. That house became more than just a place to live: it was a refuge. A little pocket of peace for me and my girl. For the first time in a long time, I could breathe. Surrounded by others, I felt less alone.

In that house was a man who made me laugh, kind in his own way. Five years later, he became the father of my son. Looking back, I don't know exactly what drew me to him; maybe it was loneliness. That was thirty-six years ago; he's gone now, but for a time, he was part of my story. Recently, a picture appeared on my memories page, showing him sitting with friends, holding our son. In that moment, I felt a tenderness towards him. In that moment, I knew there had been love.

When I welcomed my son into the world, he was exactly how I'd imagined: chubby little face, a fine fuzz of strawberry-blonde hair. I held him in my arms and couldn't believe he was finally here. I was scared to raise two children in a world that wasn't kind to people like us. We lived paycheck to paycheck, making do with what we had.

But the love I felt for him was fierce, stronger than any fear or anything life could throw at me.

In that moment, I knew I could give my children a life full of love, even if I didn't have much else to offer.

His father was a good man, but not especially ambitious. He wasted money we didn't have instead of providing for the family. Being with him became a kind of escape, a shield that kept the monster at bay. Survival soon became the focus. Feeding and clothing my children was the only thing that mattered.

I knew I had to take responsibility for my own choices.

With no money, no independence, and barely any work experience, I had to start moving in a new direction.

After I left my son's father, I found myself single and slowly rediscovering who I was.

Breakups are never easy, but at twenty-four, I felt a quiet kind of freedom.

I fell in with a new group of friends. Friday nights became a ritual involving campfires, drinks, and the kind of laughter that only comes from people who know struggle but choose joy anyway. The nights had a slight chill, but nothing could dampen the warmth of the fire or the people gathered around it.

The sky above was a canvas of stars, and as the embers floated up into the night, it felt like anything was possible.

In that crowd was Dave.

He had an easy smile and a kind of energy that drew people in.

His mates were rough around the edges, but fun, and decent in their own way.

It didn't take long for Dave and me to connect.

What started as a fling slowly deepened. We didn't care what we called it. We just lived in the moment.

That summer felt endless.

If someone had told me back then that this thing – one of those summer stories – would spark a decades-long friendship, I wouldn't have believed it.

The chemistry never really faded, even as we stayed just friends for years. It might've started short and sweet, but it left a mark.

1990 23A Hefron Way, Parmelia

Somehow, in that summer, amidst the crackle of the fire and the buzz of youth, a bond was formed, one neither of us could have imagined would stand the test of time.

And in some ways, I think part of us never really left that summer behind.

We kept those early days between us. It wasn't something we had to hide, but some things are just better left unsaid. Regardless of where life took us, we'd catch up, hang out, and be completely comfortable in each other's company.

He was always there to listen, and I loved hearing about his life and how things were going. We'd give each other advice, share stories, and laugh about nothing in particular. We were lucky – not everyone gets a friend like that. And throughout this, we always remained just friends.

I didn't have it all figured out, not even close. But I was starting to understand who I was after everything I'd been through. Not because of it, but in spite of it. And that was something. It was enough to keep me going.

Life kept moving, as it always does. I was still so young, and I'd already been through more than most do in a lifetime.

I didn't know then that my path would soon cross with someone else, someone who would change the course of everything.

But that's another story.

Chapter 2

Joe: The Man

Joe's life began in an extraordinary way.

He was born the day his mother arrived in Fremantle from Sicily, Italy. As the eldest son, he held a special place in the family, though he was technically the second-born. Their first child, also a boy, had tragically died in infancy, a loss that left a lasting mark. Joe grew up with one younger brother, Charlie, a brother he spent most of his life looking out for.

Giuseppe (Joe) and Camelo (Charlie) Giglia.

Joe came from a strong Italian family, and like most Italian homes, the mother was the heart of it. She migrated to Australia in the 1950s, a journey that took four to five weeks by boat, and she made it eight months pregnant. As a mother myself, I can't imagine how hot and uncomfortable that must have been, sailing into the unknown, her body heavy, probably seasick, unable to speak the language. It was a new beginning, but it must've been terrifying.

Joe always said his mum was kind, kept to herself, and was happiest at home with her husband and her boys.

Years later, when we were together, Joe's mum fell seriously ill. One day, she got a terrible headache. His brother rushed her to the hospital, and they found a blood clot in her brain. She fell into a coma and remained that way for nearly a decade.

Leone and Angelina Giglia with son Giuseppe as a baby.

I only ever saw Joe cry once, and it was then. I remember him sitting on the edge of the bed, head in hands, weeping.

"I should've stopped and said hello," he said. "I told myself I was too busy."

That sort of regret sticks.

It was a cruel way for her to live out her final years. Joe visited her religiously, year after year, never missing a visit. We'd go to the nursing home, and he'd bring a carnation and hold it under her nose. And every time, I swear her head would twitch ever so slightly, like she knew it was him. One day, a single tear rolled down her cheek. Joe gently wiped it away, kissed her face, and whispered, "It's okay, Mama. It's okay, Mama."

He missed her cooking more than anything. The big bowls of pasta, the way she'd feed him up like he hadn't eaten in days. That's what happens when someone dies. You don't just miss them, you miss everything. The food, the smells, the voices, the way they held the family together. And sometimes, when they go, the culture fades too. Things fall apart a little. I see that more clearly now.

Joe believed firmly in traditional gender roles, asserting his dominance as the unquestioned head of the family. His views were rigid. There was no space for compromise, no room for grey.

He came from a hardworking culture and took pride in providing for us. No matter how much he'd drunk the night before or how little sleep he'd had, he showed up for work. His colleagues became like extended family; they saw the reliable, joking, hardworking side of him.

That was one side of Joe. At home, he was both protective and unpredictable. He spoke his mind and lived unapologetically, regardless of the fallout. He was full of contradictions, harsh and magnetic, loving and reckless. That's what made him so human.

He carried a hard-earned toughness from five years in Fremantle Prison as a young man, a crucible that taught him resilience and sharpened his wit. It gave him the ability to read people with remarkable precision and planted the seed of his love for country music. Each lyric offered comfort during those hard years.

From the age of nineteen until his death at sixty-one, Joe battled a long, difficult heroin addiction, a chronic illness that shaped his life in ways most people will never understand.

It would be easy to reduce someone like Joe to a stereotype, to see only the addiction, not the man. But addiction wasn't the whole story. It never cancelled out the way he loved. If anything, it demanded a deeper kind of commitment from both of us, one where standing by each other meant weathering every storm, no matter how rough.

Back then, heroin was everywhere, cheap, strong, and easy to get. It swept through the '70s and '80s like a wave, and people like Joe got caught up in it. The system wasn't built to deal with it, and by the time they realised how bad it was, too many were already hooked. There weren't enough resources, not enough help.

When I met Joe, his addiction was part of his life, though he was still highly functional. He held down work and provided for us, but the drug shaped things. I wouldn't fully understand its weight until much later.

What I did come to realise was that while Joe could love deeply and care fiercely, he often struggled to be emotionally present. He wasn't cold, far from it, but at times, detachment settled in. And over time, especially when life became heavy, that distance grew harder to ignore.

I hadn't known Joe back then, not personally. But I remember how it all began.

One night, I was out for drinks at the Kwinana Hotel with a girlfriend. I wasn't expecting to see him. The bar was rough, reeking of smoke and stale beer that clung to the brown-and-orange carpet. The furniture hadn't changed since the '70s, cracked vinyl chairs and chipped tables.

Joe was just one of the guys in the pub that night, loud, confident, surrounded by mates. He was the man.

I noticed him straight away: tall, dark, and handsome, a cliché, sure, but it fit. Only later did I learn how easily he got what he wanted. That night, he walked right up to me like it was the most natural thing in the world.

From the corner of my eye, I saw him coming, and my heart jumped. Part of me braced for something cruel, maybe a dig about his ex, or a confrontation because I was her friend, but he wasn't interested in that. He was looking at me.

He stood close. I caught the scent of his aftershave. Bold, expensive. The same one he'd wear for the rest of his life. That scent became him. Even now, it takes me back.

Then came his voice.

"What are you drinking?"

I stammered, "Jacks and Coke."

And just like that, we slipped into one of those easy conversations that seem to float by without effort.

Before long, four of us were heading to Tarantella's nightclub. Tucked into Fremantle's backstreets, it was marked by a glowing red neon sign and a reputation for late-night chaos.

Inside, disco lights flashed across a sticky dance floor. A topless woman danced in a cage overhead. Drinks spilled, people slurred. It was the kind of place you went when the pubs closed, for pick-ups, deals, or company.

Just around the corner was Southside Tattoo, run by the late Bobby Thornton, the first registered tattooist in Western Australia, and a legend. He'd honed his craft behind the walls of

Fremantle Prison.

Bobby tattooed both skin and cell walls. His phoenix mural still lives on today. Joe used to run the book inside, taking bets, Tim Tams, cigarettes, whatever you had.

Everyone had a Bobby story, or at least a cousin with a dragon tattoo from him. Perth's circles were small, and ink ran deep.

That parlour thrived on late-night decisions, the kind fuelled by booze, drugs, or impulse. Outside, men lingered by the walls, waiting their turn or trying their luck. Payment wasn't always cash.

However, Joe's advances continued as the night went on. He kept throwing out cheeky lines, some smooth, some ridiculous.

Kwinana was a working-class town about forty kilometres south of Perth, built on oil refineries, chemical plants and affordable housing. Most people had a story that linked them to someone else – an ex, a workmate, a neighbour. The place was tangled. Everyone knew everyone.

With Kwinana being such a small place, people were bound to have something to say if this relationship continued. Still, when Joe came into my life, it felt like a small door had opened that I hadn't known was there.

He was charming and handsome, which both pulled me in and made me wary. His gestures were big, long phone calls, surprise gifts, and grand declarations. It was a whirlwind.

As we settled into family life, I wanted to believe his promises, not just for me, but for the kids, too. Joe was determined to make us feel special.

Joe and I at the old farmhouse in Baldivis 1993

One afternoon, he took us to the foreshore and surprised the kids with a helicopter ride. An extravagant gesture that made our usual beach trips seem small. I can still see their wide eyes, hair whipped by the wind, laughter cutting through the salty air as the chopper lifted. I stood on the sand, breeze in my face, watching their joy, hoping this was the beginning of something better.

Even then, hope sat beside doubt. His drug use and unpredictability were hard to ignore.

Life had already been a struggle, and part of me just wanted something survivable. I convinced myself this could be enough.

Through the struggle, we did move forward. We found our own kind of love, not always easy, but it was ours.

Joe never really proposed. There was no grand gesture. It just kind of happened – he wanted a child, and I wanted marriage. We never said it out loud, but somehow that was enough to move forward.

The next thing I knew, we were standing there on our wedding day. My dearest lifelong friends, Denise and Moira, stood beside me as they always had, steady, joyful, and happy for me. They knew this was something I truly wanted, and their friendship and support made the day feel even more meaningful. We were gathered in a quiet, chilly park, the kind of place where families came with picnic rugs and footies. The air had a sharpness to it, and the thin lace of their matching maroon dresses offered little protection. My dress, though white, was made from the same delicate lace, just as beautiful. We each held simple bunches of soft pink and deep maroon carnations.

Photos were taken on a little wooden bridge that arched gently over a trickling stream, the kind of rustic spot that made everything feel perfect. In the meantime, my eight-year-old son, ever the adventurous type, was climbing the nearest tree or leaning dangerously over the bridge. The photographer, clearly determined to get every possible angle, was taking his sweet time. Between Joe's growing impatience and Frank's antics, I'm surprised someone didn't end up in the stream.

And there, as always, was Dave, standing quietly with his current partner to the side, watching and waiting, a steady part of our lives. With a thoughtful smile on his lips, he took it all in. He expressed how glad he was that Joe would be able to give me everything I ever wanted, and that I was the person who could help Joe settle down. He felt honoured to witness his friends celebrating, just as we felt grateful to have him by our side, especially in a year that would bring so much change for us, a year that tested the foundation of our marriage: the birth of a child, indiscretions, and a love that was both secure and challenging.

I was already three months pregnant when we got married. Things were moving quickly, and I was trying to hold everything together. The kids, the relationship, the changes ahead.

Wedding day May 10th 1997
Smart Park Spearwood W.A

The pregnancy was difficult, emotionally more than anything. Joe's behaviour didn't shift much, and I often felt like I was navigating it alone.

I remember one day, heavily pregnant, we were meant to take the kids out to the Waroona Show. We got as far as the Medina Tavern. Joe ran in to place a bet, then came back out and said, "I'm not coming. You go. Some of my old mates are there, I want to catch up with them."

I just looked at him. I was upset. It was a 130-kilometre round trip, and I was eight months pregnant. Anything could've happened. But the kids were so excited.

After sitting there a moment, composing myself, I thought, *I'll take them.*

It was a long, exhausting drive. By the time we arrived, I was already exhausted. I waddled around the Showgrounds in the heat, bought the show bags, let the kids have a few rides, and pushed through as best I could. Then came the long drive home, every bit of me aching. I did it for the kids, and I'm sure they had a good time, but it was far from enjoyable for me.

Moments like that made me feel like I wasn't his first priority. Even in those later months, while he'd improved in some ways, the old patterns were still there.

Looking back, I don't know how much love I truly felt, or maybe I just couldn't admit it to myself at the time. Still, babies don't wait for the perfect moment. When they're ready to enter the world, they come, ready or not.

Sure enough, we welcomed a beautiful baby girl with soft hazelnut skin, deep dark eyes, just like her dad

Her arrival lit us up with warmth, love, and a kind of joy that pulled our slightly fractured family closer.

Joe was immensely proud to name her after his mum, honouring where he came from and who he loved.

He tried to change for that little girl, and in many ways, he did.

She was his pride and joy. His soft spot in an otherwise hardened world.

By then, though, my Medicare card looked more like a list of one-night stands than a family tree, not the legacy I'd dreamed of.

So many times before, the men in my life had walked away. Or maybe I ran.

But Joe didn't walk away.

He stayed. He tried. He provided.

He showed up in ways others hadn't, and that counted for something, even when I still felt like I was holding all the pieces while everything around me was falling apart.

He loved our daughter deeply.

And he loved my children from previous relationships like they were his own.

It took me a while to stop being so independent and let Joe take care of me.

He could be overly generous, handing out $50 notes like confetti, but he could also disappear for days, leaving me with nothing but worry.

I remember one winter evening, coming home from work to the old farmhouse.

Still in my stockings and heeled shoes, I was out in the paddock gathering bits of wood in the cold, just to get the stove going and warm the room.

I was fuming. My temper alone could've heated that house.

That kind of resentment builds slowly over time, even when you love someone.

That was life with Joe.

One minute, he would give you everything, the next, you couldn't even find him.

It wasn't until we built our home on the Baldivis property in 2008, 'The Farm', we called it, that I felt a flicker of hope for our future.

The house was more than a roof over our heads. It felt like a promise. Something solid. Something we both needed.

It was filled with signs of Joe's care.

He made sure we lacked nothing. We travelled the world, owned homes, drove nice cars, and had the finer things in life.

But love isn't measured in bricks and mortar.

And even as he built us a beautiful life, I could feel him slipping away.

Our blended family brought its own complications. Joe's eldest son, the oldest of all the kids, was deeply loved by Joe. However, their relationship carried tension and pressure, which often spilled into our home.

It added another layer to a marriage already carrying so much.

And during those long stretches while Joe was away, things at the farm got harder. The kind of hard you don't forget.

Sometimes I was angry too. That he could leave, and leave me there alone.

Joe's job took him away for four weeks at a time, and home for only one.

That rhythm strained our connection.

But maybe, in a strange way, it also saved it.

The time apart masked what we were losing.

It wasn't one dramatic thing that broke us.

We simply drifted.

Bit by bit.

Until one day, I realised the closeness we once had no longer felt right.

And beneath all the comforts – the house, the travels, the life – I began to feel hollow.

Not from his absence.

But from the deeper ache of feeling unseen.

I'd spent years trying to hold it all together.

Through Joe's emotional withdrawal.

Through the addiction.

Through the slow burn of my loneliness.

I still loved him. But the cracks had settled in.

In those moments of quiet despair, when the silence became too heavy, I found myself turning to Dave.

I remember one time when Joe hadn't spoken to me for two weeks.

Not a word.

I'd come in after work – no hello.

He'd go straight to the shower, then sit in the lounge, turn on the TV, and watch the news in silence.

I'd serve his dinner – no thank you.

Then he'd get up. Go to bed.

No goodnight.

No goodbye in the morning.

And then it would start all over again.

We lived in the same house like strangers.

It was as if I didn't exist.

The absence wasn't just cold.

It was cruel.

One afternoon, when it all got too much, I went to Dave.

I was worn down – not just tired, but done.

He didn't need details.

He just said, "You know what he's like." Then, "Come on, I'll take you out for a bit."

We put the kids in the car – my youngest daughter and the two grandkids – and headed up to Cottesloe to look at the sand sculptures.

While they played, we sat on the beach, watching the waves roll in.

I reached for his hand, and he didn't pull away.

He just let it stay there. Solid warm. Like he knew I needed something steady to hold on to.

After a while, he said, "It's going to be okay."

And I wanted to believe him.

God, I wanted to.

I tried not to cry.

But it was impossible, sitting next to someone who actually saw me.

Not because he had to.

Just because he did.

And in that moment, my hand in his, the sea rolling in, I didn't feel invisible.

Not for the first time in a long, long while.

Later, as he dropped me home, he said, "You know I'm here, right? Just ring me. Come over. Whenever."

It wasn't a declaration.

But it was something.

A space.

A door opened.

I kept telling myself the disconnection at home was the addiction.

That it wasn't really Joe.

I needed to believe that.

But knowing didn't make it hurt any less.

And in the end, I realised … the addiction's hold on him was too tight.

He wasn't ever coming back.

Chapter 3

Dave

Dave was a cheeky youngest brother, always up to something. Diane, the eldest, naturally took on the older sister role, part protector, part bossy, but always with love. Elaine, softer in nature, was more maternal, the one who would hug him when he cried or whisper reassurances when he got into trouble.

Being the only boy and the baby of the family, he was spoiled with attention. His mum absolutely doted on him; to her, he could do no wrong. Even as an adult, she could often be heard saying,

"Not my David, he wouldn't do that.'

Still, he was raised with love, taught good manners, and brought up to be respectful. Their Scottish culture meant the home was often filled with gatherings, where drinking and lively parties were simply part of life. When Dave was young, his parents separated and eventually divorced. Though the family dynamics shifted, the cultural atmosphere stayed much the same.

In his late teens, in June 1982, Dave lost his father in a tragic car accident, the kind of loss that sent ripples through both his family and the wider community. The men, members of the Kwinana Pool Club, had been on their way home from a night competition in Riverton. Three of them never made it home.

Among the lives lost was Dave's dad. He was just fifty-four. Beloved men were taken that night, fathers, brothers, sons, and mates. The community grieved them all.

The newspaper described Dave's dad as "one of Kwinana's best-known identities, a man who had lived in the area for years. A skilled carpenter."

I never got to meet him, but I often wished I had. If he were anything like Dave, I'm sure I would've loved him too. His daughters still carry pieces of him, quiet and proud.

Dave, roughly 16 years old. Taken in the early 1980s.

And Dave…

Well, Dave was his son. Without this man, there would've been no Dave. And without Dave, a part of me would still be missing.

Dave would sometimes shake his head and say, "Hell, that day, I went to three different funerals."

He was just seventeen.

Losing his father at such a crucial stage in life left a deep and lasting impact. Dave missed him every single day. The hurt he carried never truly faded; it lived quietly inside him, shaping who he became.

Dave's stepfather had already been in the picture by the time he lost his dad. He'd come into Dave's life when he was still just a boy, and over time, his presence began to chip away at Dave's confidence. Instead of feeling supported, Dave grew unsure of himself, insecure and often doubting his worth. That pattern followed him into adulthood and shaped the way he saw himself.

Their relationship was complicated. A constant push and pull between love and resentment. There were moments of warmth, even care, but far more often, Dave was left feeling angry, unworthy, and sometimes utterly forlorn. Still, he loved the man who had stepped in to raise him, but that love didn't stop the hurt.

The relationship was further complicated when, many years later, Dave lost his mum. It was in that moment, surrounded by the grief of her absence, that the unresolved feelings began to surface. Just before she passed, she had looked Dave in the eyes and said, "These are for you, son, when I'm gone."

She touched the jewellery on her neck and hands. Those words held so much weight, a promise that was etched in his heart. As time passed, he struggled with the deep-seated resentment towards his stepfather for failing to honour that wish. Despite this, Dave's steadfast nature compelled him to keep a solemn promise to his mum and call his stepfather every night. The ritual was a bittersweet, quiet testament to a bond and love shared for his mum.

Dave struggled with addiction throughout his life. Drugs, cigarettes, and alcohol all took their toll. It wasn't just the substances; it was the lifestyle that came with them. He made reckless decisions, lost thousands of hard-earned dollars, and watched his relationships and health, both physical and mental, fall apart.

In the end, I like to believe that we found a way to face the pain, even if we couldn't fix the addiction. After all, love is a powerful medicine.

Decades of research now suggest that instead of focusing only on addiction, we should ask about the pain that lies beneath it. In Dave's case, the harsh treatment from his stepfather left him feeling small and undeserving. The death of his father during such a formative time only deepened those wounds, which would follow him through life.

Joe, too, had faced his own challenges. Mistreated by his father, he carried a quiet suffering that showed itself through addiction. It was a pattern that seemed to echo through generations, as though pain had been handed down like an unwanted inheritance.

If we learned to treat the pain rather than just the problem, maybe fewer lives would be lost, not just in death, but in the slow unravelling of those who never find their way back.

Dave could be erratic, always on the go, deeply aware but often unfocused. He had a true party spirit, the kind of bloke who brought a bit of light with him wherever he went. Some of his happiest days were spent working alongside his mum at the Waikiki Hotel in Western Australia.

He started working young, rising before the sun to help in the stables. The smell of fresh hay and the soft neigh of horses became part of his daily rhythm. People often said that both children and stray creatures were drawn to him, as if they could sense the kindness in his heart. Whether it was a skittish foal or an injured bird, Dave always offered a gentle hand, a quiet reflection of the goodness he carried within.

That same dedication followed Dave into the construction industry. He often worked alongside his Scottish family friends, sometimes even on the same job sites as Joe, around the Cockburn and Kwinana areas. As a machine operator, he took pride in the sweat and skill it took to build roads and structures. It was one of the few places where he could focus, work hard, and feel a sense of worth.

I had known Dave long before I met my husband, and he had known Joe even longer. Ten years younger, Dave looked up to Joe as a mentor, a father figure, and a true friend. Despite his big heart and strong work ethic, Dave was always searching for reassurance, for connection, for the kind of friendship that didn't come with conditions.

That friendship came with Joe. He didn't judge Dave; he just accepted him as he was. Joe watched out for him, even when Dave's constant mishaps and restless energy rattled him. He'd often say, "Not many people rattle me, but he's one of them. I don't know how you cope with him."

One afternoon, we were all out the back, the kids splashing in the pool, when Dave started throwing a rubber snake at Joe, who was terrified of snakes. Joe snapped. He grabbed the rubber snake and started whacking Dave with it, over and over, like he was a naughty child. I was sitting under the patio, watching it unfold, and I felt like the parent of both of them. I yelled, "Joe, stop that!"

Dave just laughed and took it, unfazed. Joe stormed off into the house muttering, and Dave went back to playing in the pool with the kids as if nothing had happened.

Sometimes, when Dave got a bit too much, Joe was almost relieved when the two of us did our own thing. Through everything, they stuck by each other. Years of history, a lot of laughs. It wasn't perfect, but they always showed up for each other.

Dave was also a proud Pop. He'd stand on the sidelines at footy games, shouting encouragement until his voice was hoarse, his face lighting up every time they touched the ball. His pride in them was unmistakable.

As the years passed and they grew older, he treasured the moments when they'd drop by his unit unexpectedly. He'd grin, eyes crinkling at the corners, as he pulled them in for a hug.

When illness took hold, he found it increasingly difficult to maintain personal relationships, and as a result, these visits became less frequent. That never meant his love faded. It remained constant.

Any child who became part of Dave's life was lucky to have known him. My children and grandchildren were among those who built their own unique bonds with him over the years.

Despite everything, the lifestyle, the choices, the wild days, there was one unwavering presence in Dave's life: his mother.

No matter where he was or what he was doing, he always checked in on her. He loved her deeply, and when she passed, it left a quiet ache that stayed with him for the rest of his life.

In his unit, he created a small shrine in her memory, always keeping fresh rosemary in a little vase, the earthy fragrance filling the room. One day, while browsing an op shop, he found a trinket with a poem about mothers and placed it beside the rosemary, a quiet tribute to the woman he missed so much.

Dave passed away three years after his mum. Losing him was devastating, but I take comfort in knowing he would have been overjoyed to be reunited with his parents.

Dave's parents, David & Sylvia

Chapter 4

Lines Crossed

When Joe took on FIFO life, the farm settled into a quieter rhythm, embracing an easier stillness. The whirlwind of his presence, the chaos that once trailed him, had finally eased. The turbulence that used to follow me home had lifted, replaced by a calm I wasn't quite used to.

Driving down the long, dusty limestone driveway, I'd catch sight of the jacaranda tree in full bloom, its branches heavy with vibrant purple flowers. Petals drifted lazily to the ground, carpeting the earth in a soft, violet haze. The scent of warm eucalyptus mixed with the faint sweetness of blossoms in the air, a reminder that the seasons were shifting, just as my life had.

Routine became simpler. There was no rush, no unpredictable outbursts waiting behind the door. Evenings were steady: dinner, then a quiet moment watching Home and Away, our new school night norm. Sometimes, I'd sit on the verandah, the cool night air against my skin, listening to the low, rhythmic croak of the frogs and the distant call of an owl hidden somewhere in the trees. I'd wrap my cardigan tighter – comfort in solitude.

Throughout the years, I found that most nights I wasn't alone. If it wasn't one of the kids staying on the property, it might've been a family friend, or Dave, who, at times, lived there, but always seemed to be around regardless.

There was always a comforting presence that kept things from feeling too still. Maybe one of the adult kids staying in the old farmhouse, their laughter drifting across the yard. Or the grandkids would race up to the car before I had even turned off the engine, their little voices tumbling over each other, eager to tell me about their day.

If it was Dave, he'd amble over at his own unhurried pace, cigarette in hand, a knowing smile already on his face.

"Hey, how was your day?" he asked, his voice low and familiar.

Just like that, the weight of the world would slip from my shoulders.

His friendship was invaluable. We'd always shared something unspoken, a bond that grew naturally. I would catch myself unintentionally watching him, sometimes as he sat lost in thought, basking in the sun while I worked in the garden. Other times, as he pulled up on the drive on his Harley, self-assured, relaxed, and perfectly in tune with the bike.

There was a ruggedness about him that I loved, yet he possessed a quiet kindness and a genuineness that felt instinctual rather than forced. He'd show acts of care that touched me in a way I didn't expect – carrying my shopping, bringing me a cool drink while I was in the garden. Sometimes, he'd just sit nearby, and it was the nearness more than the words that soothed me.

I caught myself looking at him a little longer than I should have, wondering when the line had started to blur.

Meanwhile, Joe had settled into FIFO life, and it suited him. It pulled him out of the destructive cycle he'd fallen into in suburbia, giving him a fresh start. In the red dust of the Pilbara, where he made new friends, people who had no idea about his past in Perth, it was a chance to reinvent himself, and he thrived on the positive feedback he received. These new friendships became increasingly important to him, their opinions shaping his sense of self.

He was someone different in the Pilbara, respected, easy-going. Compared to that, I felt like the neurotic wife stuck at home, the one left to deal with everything when he finally returned. The contrast between the man he was up north and the one who walked back through the door was stark.

The year was 2010, and we all settled into a new routine. Dave carried on with his usual work around the farm. One afternoon, I wandered out the front, looking for him and spotted him down at the shed, tinkering with something.

Dave wasn't big on social events, so I wasn't expecting him to want to come when I told him, "I'm going to a party tonight. It's a 50th red carpet theme. You wanna come?"

He looked up at me, holding my gaze for a few seconds before shrugging, "Yeah, sure, I'll come. Why not?"

He said it with that calm ease of his, but there was a flicker of something else, curiosity maybe, anticipation?

It wasn't the most enthusiastic response, but I was surprised he agreed at all. If he'd known what the night held, maybe he would've been a bit more excited.

"I'll have to go home, get changed, and I'll come back and pick you up around six."

"What about your girlfriend?" I asked, teasing.

He just shrugged. "She's just a roommate."

I said, with slight envy, "With benefits?"

He didn't bite. He just gave me a look, like he was saying, I'm not getting into it.

By the time he came back, I was ready, wearing my fitted Lisa Ho designer label evening dress, a lucky op shop find. I heard his familiar voice as he let himself in.

"You ready?" he called.

I turned, taking him in. He'd made an effort, not that anyone else might notice, but I did. He wore his best AC/DC shirt, worn black Levis, desert boots, and his flannel shirt. The AC/DC belt buckle gleamed under the light, a small detail that made me smile. It was just him. He had that rough-around-the-edges look, like he never tried too hard but still managed to look good.

He gave me that once-over look, his eyes scanning my dress.

"You look great! Love that dress."

I smiled, my voice rising slightly with genuine appreciation, "Thanks."

Reaching into his pocket, he added, "Got you this; wanna take it?"

I raised my eyebrows.

"I've already had some," he continued nonchalantly.

Without even thinking, I swallowed the small, white speedball, as some might call it – a small amount of amphetamine wrapped in a rollie paper. Energised, we stepped out into the evening, which promised adventure. The evening was warm, the kind of summer night where the pavement still radiated heat and the air was alive with the distant call of the kookaburras.

The party was in full swing when we arrived, jukebox pumping, lights flashing, people laughing, drinks flowing. As we stepped inside, Dave leaned in, whispering, "Let's not stay all night."

I nodded, my gaze sweeping across the crowd of unfamiliar faces, a flutter of unease rising, maybe from the speed we'd taken earlier. Seeking familiarity, we stuck close to each other. I could tell he was out of his depth, so I made a point of staying by his side.

The relentless noise and pulsing chaos of the party became too much. We decided to escape. We drove around aimlessly until we found an empty oval and pulled over. When Dave turned off the engine, the sudden silence felt almost deafening.

We were two people who were rarely quiet, suddenly swallowed by the stillness.

The night air was thick with unspoken thoughts. My heart pounded as I tapped my fingers against my leg, unsure of what to say. Dave got out of the car and lit a cigarette. The glow briefly lit up the angles of his face as he began pacing, taking slow, steady drags.

After a few measured steps, he stopped and looked at me, really looked at me, and gave a small, slightly determined smile,

"Let's go back to the party," he said.

By the time we returned, the party had quietened down and was winding to a close. My friend offered us the spare pull-out lounge to crash on, and we both accepted without hesitation. Maybe subconsciously, we sought the comfort of being together, even if we hadn't said it out loud yet. As we prepared to settle in, I hesitated for a moment before asking quietly, "Is it okay if I sleep with you tonight?"

My words hung in the silence, simple yet laden with meaning. Dave's usual grin spread across his face as he nodded, his eyes twinkling with unspoken understanding.

The moment we were alone, there was no hesitation. Years of chemistry, of orbiting each other and an unspoken attraction, finally pulled us together. Frustration, desperation, loneliness or maybe the cloud of alcohol and drugs, all pushed us towards something inevitable.

It wasn't slow or tender, not like a love scene from a movie. It was urgent, fierce, and consuming – a release, a relief, and recognition of something we had always known but never acted on. There was a desperation to it, like trying to make up for time silently lost.

With every movement, the connection deepened, not just physically, but in a way that went beyond words, something that had always been there, waiting. We fit. We always had.

This wasn't just passion; it was coming home. And for the next fifteen years, until his dying breath, that feeling never faded. It was always home. He was my home.

I woke with a start, heart hammering in my chest as I struggled to orient myself. The air was thick with the acrid scent of alcohol and cigarettes clinging to my skin, my clothes.

Faint light seeped through the cracks in the blinds, the first hint of sunrise creeping in. Disoriented, I fumbled in the dim room, my fingers brushing over scattered clothes as I hurried to dress.

Beside me, Dave stirred.

I nudged him.

"Wake up," I whispered.

He groaned, groggy, but moved with the same urgency. We slipped out of the house, the door clicking shut behind us.

Sliding into the car, we exchanged a glance, a shared smile, laced with excitement and something else: a flicker of nerves. This had been a long time coming, but now that the line was crossed, there was no turning back. And no doubt, there would be consequences.

The drive home was steeped in silence, the kind that carried weight, thick with meaning. As the car rolled into the long driveway, heaviness settled over me. I turned to him, my voice barely more than a whisper.

"I don't want you to go."

For a moment, he just looked at me, his expression unreadable. Then, his eyes locked onto mine.

"I'll be back, I promise."

And then he was gone, tyres spitting gravel as he roared down the driveway. I stood there, watching, as the dust swirled and settled. When I stepped back inside the house, I felt the weight of solitude settle around me. I was alone.

I walked slowly into my room and closed the door, breathing in the scent of him that lingered on my clothes as I began undressing – a reminder of our intimate night together. I stepped under the warm cascading water of the shower, letting the traces of him and the intimacy of our closeness and the passion we had shared the night before wash away.

Only a couple of hours later, though it felt much longer, I heard his car again. I saw him coming around the side of the house towards the back glass sliding door. My breath caught at the sight of him. I went to him, close to tears. The emotion of everything that had happened was overwhelming. His arms came around me. A kind of shelter, we stood like that, wrapped in an embrace. After nineteen years of keeping it as a friendship, everything had changed in a single night.

A fresh scratch marred his face, the wound a silent testimony to whatever had unfolded while he was gone. I didn't ask. He didn't explain.

He kissed me, this time with intention. The want between us had not faded, only deepened in the quiet of the morning. We sank into the lounge, tangled together, hands tracing gentle paths, exploring slowly, like we were finally allowing ourselves to feel the depth of what had always been there between us. Neither of us wanted the closeness to end. We stayed there like that, wrapped in quiet happiness. So much had shifted in just a few hours. Eventually, I untangled myself from his arms and moved to the kitchen.

He followed.

"Are you hungry?" I asked, glancing back as I put something together in the kitchen – nothing fancy, just the kind of thing you do when you want someone to stay.

That night, Dave crashed on the lounge.

I woke up the next morning, the soft glow of dawn spilling through the bedroom window. I felt a gentle smile curling at the corners of my lips. As the remnants of sleep faded, a warmth bloomed quietly in my chest, a calm I hadn't known in years, a feeling of renewed love, like the promise of spring after a long winter. Rising from bed, I wrapped myself in a light cotton robe, the familiar fabric enveloping me like a warm embrace. I took a moment to breathe in the stillness of the house. Today felt different. Today felt hopeful.

With quiet steps, I wandered down the hallway, warmth beneath my bare feet, each step drawing me closer to where he lay asleep on the lounge. His eyes were closed, a hint of dark stubble beginning to show on his face. I looked down on him, savouring those moments, drinking in the sight of him, the way his chest rose and fell with each breath, the peaceful expression on his face as if the world's troubles had momentarily faded away.

I gently touched his face, and his eyes flicked open.

"Good morning," I whispered, my voice barely louder than a breath.

He smiled, a sleepy yet genuine smile that warmed me from the inside out.

"What are you doing up so early?"

I shrugged and smiled. "Just checking you're still here."

He propped himself up on one elbow. "Of course. You can't get rid of me that easily." His expression was soft with tenderness and a definite hint of a smirk. "You're beautiful, you know."

He said that so often over the years. It took me years to accept the compliment. My cheeks flushed. Then his demeanour shifted back to his cheeky self as he added, "So are you making coffee or what?"

After that night, words weren't necessary. We were bound now, not by obligation, but by something deeper. Whether we understood it or not.

After the party, Dave stayed on my lounge more often than not. I was home with just my daughter now, and in the quiet spaces of the farmhouse, we found plenty of time for our moments. I'd lie on the wide luxurious sofa with him, watching TV, even if his taste in shows was, by all accounts, the worst. His arm would wrap around me, and with my cheek resting on his chest, I could feel the steady beat of his heart beneath my ear. The isolation of the farm only made that calm feel more profound, a quiet refuge amid everyday life.

While I cooked lunch or dinner in the expansive kitchen, with its beautiful stone bench tops and large glass windows framing the pool, I'd casually call out, "You want something to eat?"

It was completely normal for him to be there, a familiar presence as any family member. I'd watch him move about in his board shorts, shirtless, clearing leaves from the pool, the pine forest rising in the distance on the hill.

Dave was our pool boy, just like in the movies. The lady of the house fancied him.

Over the next couple of weeks, he split his time between the farm, his mum's place, and staying with his girlfriend slash roommate. He was never really clear on that. Whatever was going on, things seemed to be going downhill rapidly, with him spending less and less time there.

One day, I ventured into the home at his insistence to help him collect some of his belongings. I stepped into a sparse room, clearly not his own, just a few scattered possessions and no proper bed, just a mattress on the floor, clearly not where he was sleeping.

It wasn't so much that I was upset about him sleeping at her place. If anything, I felt sad for him. He'd admitted it was convenient they were friends; he needed somewhere to stay, a reflection of his desperate search for a place in life.

And so, for another month, the facade continued.

Dave's last outing with his "friend" was an AC/DC concert; it was just him, his friend and his nephew. At the last minute, he turned to me.

"Please come," he said. "I've got a spare ticket, come with me." I was sceptical, but I went.

The evening had a high-voltage atmosphere; you could feel it in the air. The crowd was electric, the music pumping, his nephew had somehow managed to secure wristbands, and we ended up down the front.

Amidst the excitement, there was an undercurrent of awkwardness, secret, lingering touches and tension. When it was time to go home, I could see him distancing himself from her. I felt guilt – a natural human emotion.

They dropped me home, and there was an uncomfortable silence. He looked at me with a pained glance, and I returned it. Then they left. I was left reeling with a mix of emotions.

The next day, I struggled through work, putting on a brave face. But when I got home, my heart skipped a beat. There he was, waiting for me. I felt a rush of emotions, not knowing what to expect.

He told me they'd had another argument – explosive, this time. I'm sure our part in an already volatile relationship hadn't helped. The relationship had hit its final note.

I gave him a sad smile, opened the door, and he came on in. I put the kettle on, the faint smell of coffee already curling through the air, comforting in its familiarity. His shoulder brushed mine as I passed him the remote. He flicked on the TV, and our life continued, familiar and unchanged, for now.

Dave and I
March 8th 2010
AC/DC Concert, Subiaco Oval
Perth, WA

Chapter 5

Finding Our Rhythm

Nine years is a long time to sustain an affair. These weren't just stolen moments; they were woven into the fabric of workdays, family obligations, friendships, and the quiet hum of normalcy. We didn't just meet in secrecy; we existed in plain sight, navigating a world where our love had to be carefully hidden, yet somehow still managed to thrive.

There were times of great joy, nights that felt endless. The thrill of a glance held just a little too long across a crowded room. But there were also times of deep sorrow. Moments when the weight pressed down so heavily, I felt the walls closing in. The lie was suffocating, the fear of exposure constant. There were nights I lay awake, sleep refusing to come. I'd lie there, eyes open in the dark, wishing I could walk away from my marriage, to run into Dave's arms, where I felt alive.

When I saw Dave next, I would share my feelings with him, and we'd talk it through. He always assured me that this was the best way, not just for ourselves, but for everyone involved. Even though Dave was in a relationship with me, his best friend's wife, he told me he couldn't bear it if I left Joe. There was no neat logic to it. Just raw feelings

There was always the anxiety of parting when Joe came home. Dave would make himself scarce for a few days, then quietly return. It was an excruciating way to live, balancing love and deception, but it was the only way we knew how. So it went on, year after year.

In those early years, Dave didn't have a steady girlfriend, but he did see other women, maybe for a night, a weekend, a few weeks. I hated it. I hated how it made me feel. Still, it was the truth, and leaving it out would feel like denying part of our story. We weren't exclusive. Not yet. We were still finding our rhythm, slowly forming a bond in a messy, complicated situation. Some days we just shared the everyday things, dinners, and late-night TV. It wasn't always easy. There were hiccups and heartache as we tried to figure out what this even was between us.

One evening, Dave brought a woman home to stay in his caravan, less than a hundred metres from our bedroom window. I lay awake that night, imagining him in there with her, holding her. *God,* I thought, *am I going to lose him?*

I had to hide just how much it hurt. Inside, I was screaming. *How could he do this to me when I thought he loved me?*

It forced a conversation later on.

What was this? What were we doing? Was this serious, or just another short-lived relationship?

Then I'd remember. I was married.

How could I have not seen the situation for what it was?

We'd put ourselves in a position that was, if not impossible, undeniably complicated. While I was inside playing the part of a wife, Dave was often out there alone, carrying the same anxious feelings, the same turmoil running through his mind.

Maybe I wasn't the only one hurting.

When morning finally arrived, I moved quickly, yet tried to take my time, as if it didn't matter. As if slowing down might help me make sense of it all.

I walked to the front of the house, my eyes scanning the yard, drawn to the caravan standing alone. The morning sun broke through the clouds, but it didn't brighten my mood.

The air felt heavy with the unspoken secret the caravan held.

I took deep, steady breaths, desperately trying to calm my racing heart. I felt him watching me from the van, as though he'd been waiting for my arrival. He appeared in the doorway and walked toward me with a determined stride, his gaze fixed on mine, a hint of guilt in his expression. He knew I was upset, and it weighed heavily between us.

Once he was close enough, I whispered, "Why?"

He shrugged. "I don't know. I felt bad for her."

As if that was enough, as if that explained everything.

He went on about wanting me. The more he talked, the more I realised: he had a habit of picking up women in vulnerable situations. Maybe I was one of them, too. The thought came and went, but it was there.

He looked at me with soft, searching eyes.

"No, listen to me," he insisted. "I choose you. Always. No matter what, it's you I want."

His voice caught slightly as he apologised for the pain he was causing. Dave was an emotional guy, and I felt the sincerity in his words. But I also felt the weight of the past repeating itself.

"Dave, I can't bear to go through this again," I said, my voice trembling as I fought to keep tears at bay, "It hurts too much. I've done it before with Joe. If this is what you want, go. Be with her. But you can't stay here. I'm not putting up with it. I can't."

He understood. As he walked away, I went inside, feeling a mix of relief and hurt. He had chosen me, but even in that moment, it didn't feel like a victory.

A short time later, I heard his car pull away. He didn't return until late that night. The sound of the engine fading made the house feel emptier somehow. All day I'd worried and stressed, my chest tight, hands restless, playing every scenario over in my mind, wondering if he would come back, even though I'd made my feelings clear.

That night, I lay there, finally seeing the headlights sweep down the long driveway. My breath caught. Joe was home, and I couldn't go to him. Lying in the dark, staring at the ceiling with tears I wouldn't let fall, all I could think was whether Dave felt as broken as I did. All I wanted was to go to him, to hold him, and to believe, even just for a moment, that somehow, we were going to be okay.

The next morning, while Joe was out, Dave told me it was over with her. He looked at me with regret and said quietly, "I'm so sorry. I hope you can forgive me."

I nodded, the words catching in my throat. "I get it… I'm married."

He shook his head gently. "Yeah, but I want this. I want you."

Dave had told me it was over, but it wasn't until a few days later, at the local shop, that I ran into her. She came at me loudly, drawing the attention of onlookers. She demanded to know why it mattered. She spat, her voice sharp, questioning why Dave even cared what I thought. It was a blame-filled tirade, her way of unloading the ending of their short-lived encounter.

Not long after, Dave and I decided we would be exclusive. Even though I was still married, and Joe remained in our lives, he worked a four-and-one roster, meaning he was only home for just over two years out of the nine he worked away. The rest of the time, it was just me and Dave, seven years together, mostly without Joe around.

Dave made it clear he wouldn't see anyone else, and he expected me to look to him alone for the love I needed. And I did. Over the years, I became more disconnected from Joe, but I always tried to love him. I held on, even as the space between us grew wider. When he came home, it felt like I was betraying Dave.

If anyone had known about our arrangement, it might have seemed complex or contradictory, but for us, it was simple. Over the years, we didn't feel the need to look elsewhere. We got everything we needed from each other. Somehow, we were happy.

That moment changed something in both of us. I'd still been holding onto parts of my marriage, telling myself I could keep the balance; but when that happened, I knew. I wanted him. And he wanted me. We both decided this was what we wanted: a life together. It wasn't a magic fix – there were still ups and downs – but the love was stronger, more certain.

From then on, things began to shift.

Those were years of simple, unexpected moments, when we were still finding our rhythm together. While I was studying in the city, Dave would pick me up and we'd wander through the gardens. Out of town and away from prying eyes, we could feel like a couple, even if it was just for a day. That was how we managed.

Once, after class, he bought me tulips from a quaint florist in Leederville. I didn't think much of it at the time, but when I look at the photo now, I see the smile tugging at the corner of my lips, the way it lights up my face and how much younger I felt and looked that day.

One of the most difficult times came when Dave used a payout to buy a caravan and moved to a park in Pinjarra. It wasn't local anymore, and the distance made everything harder. I was living a double life, and Pinjarra was just far enough away that visiting him took planning and stealth.

When Joe was away, it was more manageable. But when he was home, I'd finish work, race down the highway to see Dave, and then get back in time to cook dinner and keep up appearances. It was exhausting, but by then, Dave had become my priority.

Leederville 2010

Often, I'd find him unshaven, not eating, just drifting through the days. I'd walk into the caravan, the air thick and stifling from the heater running non-stop, the smell of sweat and body odour hanging in the small space. Dishes were piled high, clothes were thrown everywhere, and everything was a mess, including him. I'd push him toward the shower, open the windows to let in fresh air, wash the dishes, make his bed, and coax him to eat something. At least when I left, I knew he was clean, fed, and the space was a little lighter. Before heading off, I'd promise I'd be back. I just wanted him to know I was always there, and that I'd always make time to get to him, no matter how hard it was.

On good days, we'd collect his medication, then sit by the river opposite the Ravenswood Hotel or park by the Murray River, him fishing as I sat and reflected on the surrealness of the whole relationship.

When he finally moved closer, he brought his caravan from the park in Pinjarra and set it up at the back of his sister's house. It was a relief. I could get to him more easily, and we weren't so far apart.

His sister loved him deeply and supported us without judgment all those years, but living with Dave wasn't always easy. Some days, he was helpful, funny, and kind, pitching in around the place without being asked. Other days, the self-destructive habits took over, and he could be moody or withdrawn, making decisions that affected not only himself but his sister. The atmosphere got tense more than once. No matter how much she loved him, I think she quietly wondered how much longer she'd be able to cope with him there.

While he was living at his sister's, I started searching for something more permanent for him. I pulled together all the paperwork, gathered the doctors' reports, and got Dave onto the Homewest priority housing list. When his name finally came up, it felt like such a relief.

Dave on the unit balcony, Wellard

At last, Dave had a home of his own, a secret little unit in Wellard. He was safe, and that safety made us feel safe. We made it ours, blending his treasures with our routines until it became our sanctuary, a place we could live like a couple for a few days at a time, away from the world. My hairbrush sat in the bathroom like it belonged there. It wasn't casual anymore; it was a life we were building.

Despite everything, there were questions, so many questions, from friends, family, even strangers who occasionally commented on how close Dave and I seemed. We had an explanation for everything – a smile here, a quick change of subject there. We became fluent in pretending.

And then there was Joe, an ever-present figure in our lives. Although he didn't know the full nature of my relationship with Dave – at least, I don't believe he did – he would sometimes, whether intentionally or not, let Dave step in to take care of me emotionally, quietly allowing him to be my support when he couldn't be. It was never spoken. It just happened, like an unbroken agreement.

Sometimes, it felt almost normal: the three of us in the same room, sharing laughter and making memories. Other times, it felt like a precarious balancing act, where one misstep could bring everything crashing down.

How did we manage it?

How did we find time for each other in a life that left little room for secrets?

The truth is, we carved out space where none existed – early mornings before the world was awake, stolen lunch breaks, moments tucked between obligations. We became experts at reading the clock, sensing when we had just enough time to be ourselves. Sometimes it was easy. Other times, it felt impossible. And yet, for years, we continued, sometimes recklessly, sometimes carefully, but always drawn back to each other.

Even in all the chaos and secrecy, I realised my heart always searched for light, even in the darkness.

Chapter 6

The Gamble of Life

Before either of them left this world, both Joe and Dave were gambling men. They didn't just gamble with money, but with their health, and especially with our hearts. Loving them was like playing a high-stakes game of poker with no way to predict what the next day might bring. Life's a big bet, isn't it? And like any gamble, the people closest to you feel the stakes, the constant reminder of what could be lost.

I didn't learn to read the odds by numbers. I learned by watching the men I loved take dangerous chances with everything they had. Gambling wasn't always about horse races or flashing casino lights. Sometimes, it meant risking it all by swinging past the dealer's house after work while dinner went cold on the table. Sometimes, it was gambling on a family's love, like when he lifted a finger to the barmaid and called out, "One more for the road."

The real losses didn't show up on a card table. They showed up in the empty chair at dinner or school assemblies, in all the moments that should've mattered most.

Joe was drawn to the thrill of the track and the casino. He could disappear for days, chasing that rush. At the Medina Tavern, he was a regular, beer in hand, eyes glued to the screen, shouting, arm jerking as he urged the horses home. He wasn't just watching, he was in it, fully immersed in every stride, every win or loss.

He loved his beer, but Joe wasn't a drunk. He could hold a conversation, stand his ground, and his old-school charm put people at ease. For me, the real fear wasn't the money lost or even the nights he didn't come home. The thing I dreaded most was the lethal mix of drugs and alcohol, always keeping me on edge, waiting for a call that might never come.

And one night, it did.

It was cold. He said he was going out. I knew where. I tried to stop him.

"You're tired. It's wet. Just stay home."

But my words fell on deaf ears.

Hours later, the phone rang. Joe's voice came through slurred, barely coherent.

"Where are you?" I asked, panic rising.

"I've been in an accident."

My stomach dropped, but at least he was alive. He mumbled something about an ambulance. I begged him to put the paramedic on. A calm voice came through, explaining where they were and what had happened. Joe was conscious, but not okay.

I grabbed my keys, called Dave, and flew out the door without a second thought.

"He's hit a tree coming back from the hill; he's had too much; he nodded off," I told him, urgency in my voice.

"Where? How bad is it?" he asked.

"Bottom of Karnup Road. He's alive. I'll meet you there."

When I arrived, Joe was in the ambulance, battered but breathing. I wasn't thinking about my own safety in that moment. I jumped into the wrecked car, the smell of smoke sharp in the air. Without a thought, I started pulling things from under the seat – his wallet, keys, anything that looked incriminating – and shoved them into my pockets. Even then, scared and furious, I was still protecting him. Because I loved him.

He refused to go to the hospital, no matter how much we begged. In the end, we took him home.

But it didn't stop there. Later that night, he was in pain, struggling to breathe. I called the ambulance again. Dave and I tried everything to convince him to go, but he wouldn't listen. Not until his teenage daughter knelt beside him.

"Please, Dad. You're sick. Mum called the ambulance because she's scared. Please go."

And that's when he finally did – not for me, not for Dave, not even for himself, but for his daughter. He didn't always make the best choices, but he never stopped trying for her. Another exhausting saga. Another crack in an already fragile marriage, with Dave once again standing by me through it all.

Dave was a different kind of gambler. His bets were quieter, but no less dangerous. He was drawn to the TAB, where he could sit among people without the pressure of conversation. His gambling burned just as fiercely as Joe's, just in silence. He'd blow through a paycheque in hours, leaving behind empty cupboards, a car running on fumes, and bills piling up.

And then there was his driving. If gambling was a slow unravelling, Dave's driving was a reckless freefall. Speed wasn't just a thrill; it was a need. He'd race through town like nothing could touch him. More than once, he came back with broken bones, bruises, and blood. Sometimes it was a wrecked car, sometimes a smashed-up Harley, once even a torn spleen, each crash a reminder that one day he might not walk away.

I used to joke that he had a frequent-flyer card to the emergency room. The truth was, it wasn't funny.

I've been betting on men my whole life. For years, I thought I held the winning hand: Joe, the sure thing. And then there was Dave, slow out of the gates, the underdog, who, against all odds, came up trumps.

For a while, I thought I'd hit the jackpot. That maybe, just maybe, this was it – a life I could finally hold onto.

But now the chips are down. No more hands to play, and no winners in sight.

I gambled with my heart, and I lost it all.

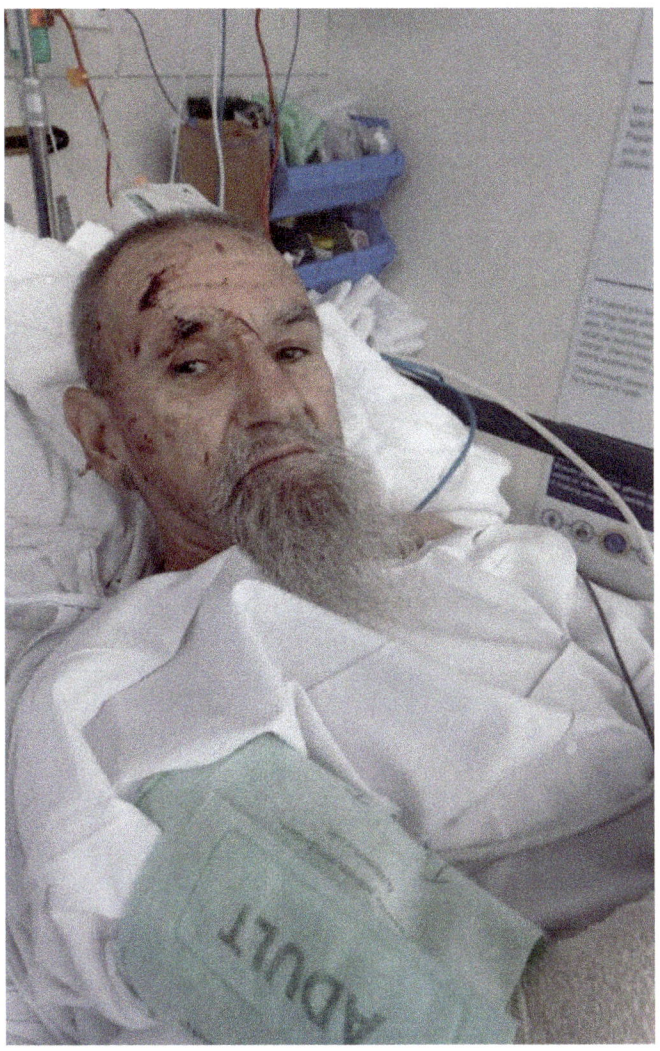

Dave hospitalised after one of his car accidents January 2024

Joe — lucky to be alive after the crash.

Chapter 7

Addiction

Addiction doesn't have a type. It doesn't care what colour your skin is, whether you're rich or poor, young or old, it just takes.

It takes trust.

It takes dignity.

Sometimes, it takes the person you love, even while they're still standing in front of you.

But the most devastating loss of all is when it takes their life.

My relationship with addiction is complicated. Not just the substances, but the struggle to understand why it chose my boys. Why did it cling to the ones I loved?

With Dave, the lines blurred. There were times I could see him genuinely trying to stay on track. Then something would shift: a phone call, a missed appointment, someone knocking at the door at an unexpected hour, and suddenly, he was gone again.

Joe's addiction was different. It wove into the rhythms of his life, almost invisible to those outside the house. He could function and work, but behind the curtain, I saw the toll it took to keep up the façade.

Me, I didn't wake up thinking about drugs or disappear for days, but that doesn't mean I didn't try to escape. Sometimes I just needed a break, a bit of peace, a way to take the edge off. It wasn't about getting high. It was about coping with a miserable day.

This isn't about blame or turning people into villains. It's about the truth. We all made questionable decisions, ones that kept us up at night, whether we spoke about them or not. Dave had his regrets. So did Joe. And me? I was just trying to hold things together the best way I knew how.

The dynamics of our relationships often caused more confusion than clarity. When we were all together, when they were just down in the shed, and I was in the house, I felt like I had some control. I could check on them, keep an eye on things. It gave me a strange kind of comfort. When they disappeared into town, that's when the fear crept in. Anything could happen out there.

When Dave and I met, he was living a wild, unanchored life, no real commitments, no steady home, just drifting from one high to the next.

Life with Dave felt euphoric, exciting, and intense. I knew what I was getting into. I'd seen it before. It mirrored parts of the life I was already living with Joe. My nature hadn't changed; I still had that instinct to fix things, to love them into becoming better versions of themselves.

At different times in my life, both Joe and Dave told me I made them better, and yeah, that made me feel good. It made me feel wanted, as though I had a purpose, like I was needed. It's softened the self-doubt I'd carried for years, made me feel like maybe I was worth something after all. However, that kind of love comes at a cost.

But being the one who 'made them better' sometimes meant carrying their chaos, too. Things could shift without warning.

One day, Dave was full of life, carefree. Next, he was unstable, waking me in a panic, convinced someone was hiding in the wardrobe. He tore the room apart. Nothing I said could talk him down. I sat in bed with my hands over my face, breathing slowly, trying not to lose it. Yelling would've only made it worse.

It was exhausting trying to bring him back to reality. Sometimes it lasted days. I'd beg him to take something to sleep, to let his brain rest, to allow himself to reset.

Throughout the years, Dave used all sorts of drugs. Mostly, it was speed. For someone already diagnosed with ADHD, that just made everything worse. He was intense. He could turn an everyday trip to the shops into a manic ordeal.

We'd walk in needing just bread and milk, but Dave would vanish down an aisle and strike up a conversation with some random bloke who'd picked up a tin of Milo. I could hear him saying, "I used to eat that straight outta the tin … still do sometimes."

Then he'd start tossing things we didn't need into the trolley, rummaging through the sales bin like it was some kind of treasure hunt. He talked a mile a minute, half to me, half to himself, and loud enough for the whole shop to hear. I'd try to steer us towards the checkout, but he'd already decided there was something he'd forgotten. Or thought he'd forgotten. Or now urgently needed, just because someone else had it in their trolley.

That was the thing with Dave: his impulses ruled him. The same way he grabbed things off the shelf, he'd grab at whatever was around in life. He was a heavy drinker and smoker, which later caused liver damage and lung disease. I always felt he just went with the flow. If someone drank, he drank. If someone used a particular drug, he used it too. He didn't seem to care what it was. The addiction was strong. He just wanted to belong.

Joe's story looked different. Like I said before, addiction doesn't care if you're rich or broke. But money? It makes all the difference. Joe was cashed up. He didn't have to beg, borrow, or steal. The dealer liked cash; he'd see Joe before the poor guy trying to swap some stolen goods for a packet.

Having that kind of money made heroin and homebake easier to get.

Homebake, a morphine-based version common in New Zealand, was central to Joe's use in the '90s. Homebake was a brownish powder, cooked up in kitchens or sheds. He even had a mate nicknamed "Cooker", for obvious reasons. Great guy though. I still wonder if he's alive today.

When Joe couldn't get homebake, he turned to what we called "boil up." It was a concentrated liquid made from leftover scrapings and alcohol, dark, thick, watery. It was what he used when he was desperate. Not choice, survival.

Boil-up came with its own damage. Joe's skin would break out in boils, especially where he injected. I'd try drawing poultices. Sometimes we would end up in an emergency, getting them lanced and packed. It was awful. All that pain, just to dull something even deeper.

Joe didn't like speed or prescription pills, and he never smoked pot. It was heroin that got its grip on him. Sometimes, he did try to beat it. Maybe because he knew it wasn't good for his health, or because it caused so many arguments between us.

We tried everything, methadone, Subutex, all the legal drugs that were supposed to stop the cravings. Some of it helped, though it also meant lining up every day. You were tied to the chemist daily.

It was near my work, and I'd often say, "Joe. Please just park across the road. I hate waiting out here. What if someone sees me? It's so embarrassing."

The stigma was heavy. He felt it too.

You'd probably run into half a dozen people in the same situation, some just waiting, some swapping, buying, doing whatever they could. It became a kind of meeting point.

In the end, he stopped going. Said he'd rather go to a mate's place to get something than line up like that every day.

Next, we tried Naltrexone, an implant from a doctor in Subiaco. You had to be completely clean before getting it, or the withdrawals would be brutal. After the implant was inserted into your stomach, you had to wait, just in case your body went into shock. The waiting room felt like a war zone: people sweating, crying, shaking. But Joe got through, not without its trauma. They'd give him some sort of prescription medication to calm him, but on the way home, he kept taking his seatbelt off and trying to get out of the car, mostly the experiences I've had on that freeway with men and drugs. I'm surprised I'm still living today.

A few weeks later, he told me, "I can't even remember what it feels like to crave heroin anymore."

It had blocked it completely, wiped out the desire, the memory, the grip it had always held on him.

Looking back, I think they should've started him on antidepressants first and counselling. The implant took away something that had been part of his whole life, and that left a huge hole.

That might be why he turned to speed, something he hadn't used before. What followed was volatile and unpredictable.

He became erratic and paranoid. Even suicidal. I remember him loading the kids in the car for a trip to the local pools; he had a gun and a baseball bat jammed down the side of the seat. I questioned him:

"What the hell do you need that for? You're not taking the kids to the pools with that shit in the car."

He just looked at me and sped off anyway.

It's no wonder I've used the phrase, "For fuck's sake," my whole life.

Speed made his thoughts race. He couldn't rest. He didn't sleep.

When the Naltrexone wore off and he went back to heroin, I was quietly relieved. After speed and all the trauma that came with it, heroin, for all its danger, felt somehow easier to cope with.

He once said to me, "I'm never gonna stop. I like it. That's just what I do."

And deep down, I knew that.

It's easy to talk about someone else's story. But what about mine?

Did I use drugs? Yes.

Did I see myself as an addict? Absolutely not.

When you're living that life, you're bound to get caught up in it, too. I suppose it just depends on how deep you go.

I often felt like everyone around me used something. But after talking to a counsellor, I discovered that only about 15% of adults in WA used illicit drugs. Some days, it felt like I knew every single one of them.

There was a time I was so depressed I could barely function. I'd given up my job. After more of Joe's indiscretions, I moved out again.

Late one night, he rang me, drunk, sad, apologetic. I went to him, like I always did. I found him in a half-stupor, the house a wreck. On a whim, he'd smashed out a wall of the old cottage, a half-thought-out renovation project in the middle of winter. Wind and rain swept straight through the place.

I tucked him into bed, told him I loved him, and started cleaning up.

That's when I found it, an eight-ball. About three grams of amphetamines, just sitting on the floor. I took it home. He didn't even notice it was gone.

Each morning, before the kids woke up, I'd tap out the tiniest line and swallow it with water. It wasn't a high; it was just enough to put one foot in front of the other. Just enough to keep breathing.

Although I'm sure no doctor would've recommended this as a coping mechanism, for that short month that worked for me, moving again.

For me, my drug of choice was marijuana. I loved it. I smoked it from about the age of sixteen into my forties. I was never much of a drinker; it doesn't agree with me. My glass of wine at the end of the day was a cone of pot. After a long day of work, I'd sit out back with my little brass pipe and my pretty trinket bowl filled with fragrant green buds of cannabis. I'd light it up just to breathe it in. The earthy smell would hit me first, the rich, almost sweet scent blending with the night air. It was a moment of calm, a small pocket of peace in my hectic life. I could feel it filling my lungs; I could feel the stress of the day melt away. The frogs croaking, the night sky above me, even in the cold. I loved those moments. My girlfriends and I would often catch up after work or on weekends, and instead of tea and biscuits, we'd have tea and cones. That was just what we did.

But as time went on, the paranoia started creeping in. I remember the last time I ever smoked marijuana. It was 2013, at the Admiral Hotel in Kwinana. A group of us had gone out, and halfway through the night, as always, someone suggested going out to the car for cones. I was hesitant: *that feeling of serenity had long since transformed into something uneasy.* But I went anyway.

Afterwards, the paranoia hit me like a jolt of electricity, sparking fear and confusion in an instant. I panicked and called Joe. I knew he and Dave were together.

"Come and get me," I said. "I want to go home."

"Why? What's happened?"

"I've been smoking, and it's made me feel terrible."

"Where are you?"

"With the girls at the pub."

"Okay, we're on our way."

My girlfriends could see I wasn't okay. I'd always been the anxious one in the group, the one who overthought everything, the one who was scared to drive in the dark. But they knew that's just how I was, and they looked out for me. They still do.

These women weren't just friends. Each of us brought something different, but together we were strong. We'd been through over forty years of life side by side – kids, then grandkids, wild nights of dancing, and the deepest losses. We've seen each other fall apart and rise again.

We were the keepers of each other's secrets. We still are.

I love them fiercely. I don't think I'd have made it through life without them.

These days, we don't party like we used to. Every now and then, we catch up for a drink, share a laugh, and look back. We've mellowed with time. But the love is still there. Always will be.

Within half an hour, Joe and Dave turned up. I was feeling awful, but at the sight of them, I felt an instant wave of relief. The pub was new, and they hadn't been there before, so for a moment, nothing else mattered. They came in and had a drink. I felt better, but the anxiety still lingered. I hovered close to them, uneasy. I think they could tell I wasn't okay. Joe took the lead: "Dave, you take her car, and we'll meet you at home." It was one of those times I really needed them, and they both stepped up.

I never smoked again after that night. I didn't want to. I grew out of it; it just wasn't my thing anymore.

Yes, I used soft drugs like marijuana and speed for about five years in my early forties, but I don't consider myself a drug addict.

Living with Joe, and later with Dave, I saw what real addiction looked like. For them, it wasn't just escape – it was survival. They couldn't function without it. That's where my comparison comes from. Some might disagree, but that's how I've always seen it.

In my life, it often felt like as soon as one problem was solved, another one showed up.

Dave's back surgery was meant to fix one problem, but it created another. The pain didn't fully go away after surgery. It got worse. He could no longer work.

Dave had worked since he was a boy. His identity was tied to being useful and providing. When that was taken, the structure of his life vanished. No more clock-ins. No knock-offs. No one to lend a hand to. Just long, empty days. No sense of accomplishment. No camaraderie. He lost his self-worth.

Maybe others noticed. But nobody lived it like I did, waking up beside him, heading to work while he stayed behind with no money, no structure, no reason to get out of bed. I saw what it did to him, day after day. He didn't just lose work. He lost part of himself. I felt for him.

After a Centrelink medical interview, they told him he could work as a parking assistant. A parking assistant! Dave, sitting in a booth all day. Didn't they read the report? Dave had ADHD. That kind of job would have driven him mad. He couldn't let it go. He ranted about it for weeks. Said he was going to blow up the office, kill somebody. I let him rant and rave, nodding and throwing in the occasional "yeah" or "mm." Not to encourage him, just enough to let him feel heard.

And then his best mate died. That was just one thing too much at this point in time.

He'd lost friends before, but this one was different. This was someone who had been around most of his life. It brought back a deeper kind of pain.

And what did he do when the pain came?

He took more drugs.

Although it was hard, we moved forward together. We healed. Some days we did well. Other days, not so good. But we kept going.

The old life no longer existed. Our relationship changed. We wanted calm. We wanted some type of future away from the turmoil we'd all lived through.

Although there were always times he fell off the wagon, he softened. The wild days faded.

As the weeks went on, our lives began to take on a new light.

Friday nights looked different now. He'd be in his bed early, propped up on his pillows. He called it his "Gold Class lounge." He had a little flat-screen TV in the bedroom, a stash of lollies and ice creams nearby. His PJ's wrapped around him. He was comfortable. Safe. Home.

It's been years since I've touched anything. But when I see people on the street, strung out, disconnected from the world, I don't judge.

I see what they're numbing.

Imagine trying to survive out there. No home. No warmth. No safety. Of course, they reach for something. Drugs dull the pain for a while, but the pain never really leaves. It waits. It lingers.

Just like it did with Joe.

Just like it did with Dave.

Drugs shaped part of their lives, in different ways, with different consequences.

But that's not what I carry now when I think of them.

I don't picture the chaos. I remember who they were underneath it all.

They were both good men.

Deeply flawed.

But deeply loved.

And somehow, I'm still here. Breathing. Healing. Carrying them with me, not as addicts. Not as broken men. But as the men I knew and loved.

Addiction shaped part of our story.

But it doesn't have the final word.

Love does.

Chapter 8

Affairs of the Heart

When it came to affairs of the heart, between me and Dave, and whoever Joe had taken a liking to at the time, there was transparency.

Dave and I kept our relationship private. We moved through life quietly and carefully. Even at home, we were mindful of appearances. In public, we acted like friends, even though we were much more than that.

That's not to say we weren't affectionate in the everyday moments, a hand on the leg while driving, and long hugs at the door after time apart. Just being near each other was enough. We didn't have to say it or show it all the time. It was just there.

So different from my relationship with Joe, where everything was out in the open, sometimes too much so. At times, it overwhelmed me. I sank into deep depression, crying more than I'd ever admit.

The betrayals had started long before Dave and I were involved. But over the years, as we talked, he came to understand just how deeply Joe's behaviour had affected me.

The whispers of infidelity weren't just in the background; they were always there, reminding me how much I was holding together, and how close I was to falling apart.

We fought.

Joe would disappear, then reappear like nothing had happened; no explanation, just a mention of a "friend" or an invite to some work event.

Once, a woman even knocked on our door in the middle of the night, asking to see him. He stayed in bed, pretending nothing was going on, leaving me to deal with a mess that wasn't mine to clean up.

The sting never dulled.

The only time I ever saw real remorse wasn't because I'd found out about another woman, it was because he thought he might lose his job.

He'd been seeing someone at work, and in a manic state, I rang his workplace demanding to speak to her. That was the moment he realised he'd crossed a line he couldn't just explain away.

When I finally stood at the door, ready to leave, he asked, "What can I do to stop you from leaving?"

I didn't scream. I didn't cry. I just said, "You're going to have to buy me a house."

It wasn't about taking him for anything. I just couldn't keep living like that, not with my daughter to think about, and nowhere else to go if things got worse.

I knew he'd never kick us out. But as much as I loved that farm, I didn't know how much longer I could keep sacrificing my mental health just to keep the peace.

He was angry, but he bought it.

I felt sorry for the real estate lady showing us through the place. Joe treated her terribly, and none of it was her fault.

Sometimes I'd stay at that house for a few days, sometimes a couple of weeks. Sometimes Dave would come and stay there with me. Then I'd go back home, thinking maybe things would change. They didn't. It was a disaster. And yet, I kept circling back, caught between hope and the man he could sometimes be.

Joe could be funny and generous when he wanted to be. He had a way of drawing people in, making them believe he was a great bloke. And sometimes, he really was …

But when he wasn't, he was a prick. Mean, nasty, sharp with his words. That side of him wore me down, bit by bit. The constant bickering, the pressure; it chipped away at me.

And when I finally snapped, I snapped. No filters. No holding back. I'd scream, swear, and slam doors.

I hated the version of me that showed up in those moments, but I couldn't always stop it.

That's what he did to me.

To explain just how far I was falling, I need to take you back, before Joe, before Dave, before any of it, when the ground first slipped out from under my feet.

That's when the self-harm began.

I don't think I ever wanted to die. It wasn't like that. I just didn't know how else to cope.

Maybe if there was something physical someone could see they'd understand how much I was hurting. I was desperate.

My mind started to spiral, like it was trying to find any kind of release from the pressure building up inside me. Back then, I was only young, maybe 23, and I was with my son's father. We were broke. No money, minimal social life, no support.

We did love each other then. There was love in that house. Neil wasn't a mean man.

But I think, in the end, it was all too much, trying to support a family with no steady job. He gave up and didn't even try anymore.

I was frustrated. Tired. How could we afford alcohol, cigarettes, and pot, but not take the kids out for the day? Not even have food in the cupboard? The house needed wood just to get hot water, and we never had any. In summer, it was boiling, no air con; no relief at all.

It was too much; I was coming apart. I'd started carrying on about everything and nothing, rambling in circles, losing the plot.

I was in the kitchen, screaming, "Is this what I've got to do? Do you want me to stab myself? Will you listen then? Will you see me then?"

And then I did it.

I picked up a knife and stabbed myself three times in the leg. It wasn't calm. It was hysterical.

The pain was excruciating, but for a moment, it drowned out the screaming in my head.

The sting in my leg became louder than everything else, louder than the fear, the anger, the exhaustion.

I could barely walk. I probably needed stitches. But I didn't go to the hospital. I wrapped it in a bandage and made up some story; I told people I fell on a star picket or got bitten by a dog.

It was easier to explain physical pain than admit how far I was falling. Maybe part of me wanted someone to finally notice. I felt completely unseen.

That afternoon, one of Neil's mates came over. He looked at me, really looked at me, and said quietly, "Are you okay?"

I just nodded and said, "I'm alright," even though I wasn't.

I wasn't brave enough to say the truth. He let it go. Didn't push, and neither did I. But in the split second, I felt seen and unseen all at once.

Fast forward to Joe, and the patterns repeated just in new ways.

There'd be a phone call. Then that sick feeling in my gut, knowing from the way he spoke that it was another woman. Then I'd react, yelling at the kids, "Get in the car, we're leaving." I'd throw stuff into the boot and speed down the driveway, not even sure where I was going or what I was doing.

And like clockwork, a couple of weeks later, Joe would follow me to wherever I'd ended up. Things would be good for a while. Then we'd argue again. He'd move out. We'd get back together.

Each move, whether to the farm or a place in Kwinana, was just another attempt to outrun the chaos.

In 2005, after another indiscretion, Joe moved back to the farm. I stayed in town, and one particular afternoon, I couldn't stop thinking about everything that had been going on.

I would get obsessive, something I still do to this day. I got into my car, in no state to be driving, and headed to the farm.

What was he doing? Who was he with? The questions wouldn't stop.

When I arrived, I saw him carrying on with his life as if nothing was wrong, joking with friends, smiling, happy, while inside I was spiralling out of control.

Then something in me snapped. In the corner, I spotted a pile of bean sticks, the ones we used to stake the runner beans.

I took one, gripping it tightly, and waited. When he stepped into view, I struck him over and over with all the force I could muster.

Looking back, was it abuse from me? Yes.

He couldn't go to work the next day because I'd bruised his ribs. He chased me, but somehow, I outran him and jumped into my car.

As he came at me, he managed to kick the side mirror off the car just as I sped away.

I'm not sure what I hoped to achieve; maybe it was just a desperate attempt to let all those pent-up feelings out.

Even now, I marvel at how out of control my behaviour has become.

I remember pulling over after sobbing so hard my body shook.

Armed with a small, sharp object, I cut into my skin: 'Joe hates me.'

It was enough to make me bleed, but it only left minimal scars, scars now covered by tattoos.

I probably should've been hospitalised in a bloody psychiatric ward. That's hard to admit, but those behaviours were nothing short of destructive.

The truth is, as broken as things were, there were still good times.

I remember nights on the farm when he'd light the bonfire, Joe walking around in his stubby shorts and old gumboots, playing the farmer. Farmer Joe. He'd pour on a little diesel – well, a lot – and when the flames roared up with a bang, we'd all jump, then laugh as he grinned, proud of himself.

There were days we'd all pitch in, picking farm-famous seedless oranges from the orchard, packing crates, loading the ute, sharp citrus in the air. Everyone was happy.

There were times when Joe was genuinely a good husband. He loved me, and I loved him. There was no doubt about the depth of our bond. But even with those moments, the relationship remained toxic.

By 2008, I was still there, doing everything for him, making sure he was safe, looking after him, giving him what he wanted and needed when he reached for me. But there was something in me that had been quiet for too long, a part that longed to feel alive in a different way.

Maybe it was the memory of better days: soft mornings on the farm, bare feet in damp grass, the sun rising over rows of beans, and a kind of silence that made me feel happy. But it never stayed that way for long, and I wanted something that would.

Maybe it was a longing for a gentler touch, or simply the desire to be loved, physically and emotionally.

By 2010, I realised I hadn't gone searching for it. Love had found me. It began as a friendship spanning years, a steady foundation that grew into something deeper. Everyone deserves happiness, and if Joe was always chasing love elsewhere, maybe he wasn't happy in our relationship either. When I began loving Dave, it was on a different level altogether. He quite literally saved my life.

Later on, as the years went by, I told him, though at first, he couldn't believe it. He didn't think his love could carry that kind of weight.

But in the end, we both knew: finding each other saved us.

I hadn't thought about self-harm in many years. It almost felt like it had never happened.

Then, recently, someone mentioned that their daughter was self-harming. Just hearing those words brought everything back in a flash, although not in the way you'd expect.

A calmness washed over me as I realised I hadn't felt that urge, or even thought about doing such a thing, since I met Dave.

No matter how much Dave drove me to the brink of distraction or exasperation, and God, he did sometimes, not once did I ever feel like hurting myself. Not once did he do anything that made my emotions spiral out of control like that.

When Dave died in 2024, the first two months afterwards were the darkest I've ever known. Only then did I truly think about taking my own life. But his constant voice in my head reminded me that I was worthy.

Only months before, I'd promised him I'd never jeopardise my own life or happiness over someone else's again.

Although that wasn't exactly how he put it, more like: "Fuck those cunts. You do what makes you happy, okay? Promise?"

I looked at him and just nodded. I know when we made that promise, we both had tears in our eyes and lumps in our throats. We knew what was coming.

Dave's love didn't just save me; it changed the way I saw myself.

Sometimes I wonder if we should've just told Joe. Just said it outright, laid it all bare. It would've caused a punch-up, for sure. Chaos. Heartbreak. But still, I wonder. All those years, pretending. Hiding. Loving in secret. What would've happened if we hadn't?

I wasn't trying to hurt anyone. Dave wasn't either. We were just … in it. Trying to survive something that already felt broken.

And yet, Joe had his secrets, too. Affairs I knew about. Others, I only found out later. I often wonder if he ever stopped to think about how much it all hurt me. If he could've said it out loud. "I know what I'm doing. I know it's killing you."

Maybe he couldn't. Maybe none of us could.

I do feel terrible for my part in the deceit; that's the truth. But I also know I couldn't have given it all away, not even for the guilt. Dave's love meant too much to me. It gave me something I didn't know I needed. Something I couldn't walk away from.

And sometimes, I wonder why Joe didn't just leave. With all those relationships, all those women. Maybe one of them could've made him happy, happier enough to be dedicated to her.

Sometimes I still wonder what might've changed if we'd handled things differently. But all the ifs and maybes in the world won't change what played out. And the truth is, we were just human. And humans, for better or worse, make complicated, messy choices when we're hurting, needing, longing to be seen.

Chapter 9

A Christmas of Too Much

Joe was home for the Christmas holidays, so we decided to take a trip down south. Well … I decided we'd take a trip.

We both did our best to keep up the illusion of a normal marriage. It wasn't much fun, but in its way, it was okay. The accommodation was stunning, with breathtaking views, a spa on the deck overlooking the forest. As always, it was a luxury – Joe wasn't the roughing-it kind of guy – a luxury Joe was more than happy to pay for, even if he couldn't resist muttering about the cost.

By the second day of our holiday, Joe was visibly unwell. He collapsed onto the lounge, eyes heavy with fatigue, fixed on the cricket. The relentless pace of his work roster, combined with questionable lifestyle choices, was taking its toll.

He wasn't engaging with either me or our daughter, so I knew exactly what I was doing when I suggested Joe ask Dave to bring something down. Dave consented for reasons he considered justifiable, and Joe sweetened the deal by promising to make it worth his while, but for me and Dave, it also meant we'd get to see each other. The whole situation was scripted. I wasn't just going along with things at that point; I had encouraged them.

Inviting Dave added another layer to the mess, but it eased some of the tension. Joe would be more relaxed, and the mood would simmer down.

When Dave showed up, the whole vibe changed. It felt easier to breathe.

The two of them did their own thing, drinking out on the deck, while I relaxed in the spa. Dave still checked in with me in small ways. "You want a drink?" he'd ask, handing me a can without waiting for an answer. Or, "You and Nini want to come for a walk and look at the emus?"

It wasn't much, just the little ways he looked after me, but it meant everything. Joe didn't like emus, but he liked cricket and beer, so he stayed inside watching the game. For now, anyway, I didn't have to be on edge. I could breathe, stretch out in the spa, and pretend, for just a moment, that I was somewhere else entirely.

The next morning, the boys drove home together in Dave's car. I didn't mind; I followed behind with my girl. The drive would be peaceful, a quiet stretch of winding country roads, offering us a bit of calm, quality time. The big Karri trees stood like sentinels along the road, their centuries of existence making them silent guardians of the land. I couldn't help but wonder …were the boys even aware of the beauty surrounding them at that moment, or were they simply focused on the destination ahead?

I liked to think that, as guardians, the trees were watching over them, protecting them from whatever lay beyond the horizon.

I knew they'd make one more stop before coming home. Joe always stocked up at Christmas, a costly mistake; the more he had, the more he would use.

By the time we got home, I could tell he'd had way too much. I looked at Dave, the tiredness draining my whole body, my face showing everything I couldn't say. I just held out my hands in despair.

"What could I do?" Dave's voice carried the same defeat I felt. "He wouldn't listen. All I could do was make sure I was there."

Joe sat slumped on the lounge, his eyes half-closed, his body sinking, his breathing slow. Then, sweats. Uncontrollable shaking.

Something was wrong.

Panic hit me.

"Joe," I said, shaking his arm. "Joe, are you okay?"

Nothing.

"Jesus, help me – kids! Dave!"

Poor bloody kids. Why did they have to go through this again? Why did I stay in an environment where my children witnessed so much trauma?

I don't know why I thought the cold shower would help, but we got him in there somehow. The ensuite was crowded, everyone pressing in, voices rising.

Later, I learned it was the worst thing I could've done. It sent him into shock. The sudden change in body temperature made everything worse. A shower won't fix an overdose. Remember that.

"Get the wheelchair!"

Someone yelled.

"We need to get him to the hospital; he can't walk!"

He was barely conscious, his body a dead weight in our hands. I slapped his face lightly, then harder.

"Come on, Joe. Stay with us. Stay awake."

"Mum!" Pania, my oldest daughter's voice cut through the chaos. "Just stop it. Let it end."

The weight of her words pressed heavily on my chest, each syllable a testament to the pain my struggles had inflicted on the kids.

I froze. My body felt heavy, drained, like all the fight had been wrung out of me.

Maybe she was right. Nothing ever changed. Even if Joe made it, the cycle would go on; he wouldn't stop. Life wouldn't magically shift. I was just surviving inside a marriage that had already ended, stuck in a place that kept swallowing me whole.

But even as that truth crushed me, something deeper refused to let go. I couldn't let his life slip away. Not like this. Not when there was still a small part of me that hoped.

I swallowed hard, "No!"

Somehow, we got him into the car. I don't know who drove. I don't know how we got there. I just remember we did.

The stigma of taking someone to the hospital for an overdose is significant. I felt embarrassed, humiliated, and patronised, as though I was the one at fault, despite trying to save a life.

The tone was condescending: "Has he taken drugs? What sort? Do you know what that can do to you?"

As if I didn't, the stupid bitch, of course I did, I lived it every day. I wasn't treated as someone seeking help, but as someone to be judged. It was unfair. This situation was beyond my control.

Joe was in the hospital for two weeks, one of them in intensive care.

It turned out it wasn't an overdose this time, but a dirty syringe that nearly killed him. He developed sepsis, a life-threatening infection that travelled through his bloodstream and into his spine. I had to notify the family, just in case he didn't make it. Thankfully, he did. When it was time to go home, they told me he couldn't; he'd need an intravenous drip, and they didn't allow addicts to go home with drips. It was said matter-of-factly, but it landed like judgment.

No matter what I did or how close we'd come to losing him, there was always that tone in the air, as if I was supposed to be ashamed.

Those two weeks drained everything from me. My body ached. My eyes burned from exhaustion. But I stayed, watching over Joe, holding his hand, comforting him. Holding the family together.

And amidst all this chaos stood Dave, steady and real.

"You okay?" he'd ask, his voice low, drawing me into his arms.

I'd nod, even when I wasn't. If it weren't for him pulling me up, keeping my head above water, I think I would've drowned.

I lived my life constantly on edge, terrified that one day Joe wouldn't come home.

When he recovered, he'd return to me with softness, his voice filled with remorse, love, and sincerity.

"I don't know what I'd do without you, love. I would've been dead years ago if it weren't for you."

He'd envelop me in one of his giant bear hugs, nearly crushing me as he professed his love. In those moments, I never doubted his affection. It was there, buried under everything else – but it was real. And I loved him. I didn't want him to die.

Joe's addiction led me into co-dependency. I enabled him, even as I lost sight of myself.

The scariest part wasn't the turmoil. It was how easily I could return to normal, how I'd pour the tea the next morning and act like none of it happened.

Chapter 10

Birthday Love

As the big day approached, my 50th and Joe's 60th, I felt that familiar mix of excitement and dread. I wanted it to be perfect. But underneath all the planning sat the same old tension: keeping Joe in the right frame of mind.

That morning, as we woke up side by side, the first words slipped out of me without much thought.

"If you're gonna go out, go now," I said. "If you need to do stuff, get the paper, whatever it is, do it now. You need to be back this afternoon."

I wasn't giving permission. I was acknowledging what we both knew but never said aloud: he'd probably want to score before the party. It was my way of trying to manage the day. If he went early, got it out of the way, maybe the rest of it would run smoothly.

His mood, his presence, the tone of the whole night hung on that fragile balance. More than the decorations or the food, that was the real work.

Later that afternoon, after the rain had stopped, Joe decided to go for a ride on his bike. He pulled on his thick black leather jacket and helmet. His Harley gleamed as if it were brand new, polished to perfection in the shed. Proud as a kid with a new pushbike, he revved the engine and roared off, water spraying from the back tyre. The roads were still wet, and I worried as I called out, half-joking, half-serious:

"Don't be long. Be careful."

I stood at the end of the driveway, watching the road and the clock.

I'd done everything to make it right. The costumes were laid out on the bed, cowboy hats to match, and the country band was set to arrive at seven. Down in the shed, the spit roast was already slowly cooking, the smell of meat drifting across the yard.

Looking back, I can see how deep the codependency ran. It wasn't the textbook picture of enabling addiction. It was quieter than that, hidden in the details, me believing that if I could just keep things "right," the night would be okay. That we'd all be okay.

Joe was proud that day. Sixty years old, he'd worked hard his whole life, and he deserved to celebrate. He'd bought himself a Harley Davidson CVO Limited Edition, bronze, not black, gleaming in the sun. He loved the colour, loved the attention.

The boys all gathered in the shed, watching as he kicked it over. The engine roared, his grin stretched wide, and he was in his element. I was proud of him, too, proud of all he had achieved.

The night rolled on with music, laughter, food, and plenty of photos. Someone took one of the three of us: Joe, Dave, and me, arms wrapped around each other.

When I look at it now, I can still feel the weight of Dave's arm draped over my shoulder. The scent of fresh rain hung in the air, mingling with the warmth of red wine on his breath. A cigarette sat forgotten between his fingers. No one else knew about the bond between us, but I see it in the way he stood close, his presence wrapped around me like a secret.

That photo didn't just capture a party. It held the story of us, Joe, Dave, and me. A moment frozen in time where I felt nothing but love and protection from them both.

That night felt easy. No tension, no drama. Surrounded by friends and family, I could brush against Dave's arm or stand close without raising suspicion. It felt natural.

I remember him drinking, not recklessly, just freely. But it caught up with him. His words slurred slightly.

"I need to lie down."

I guided him into the spare room, pulled off his boots, and tucked the blankets over his shoulders. He looked up at me, eyes glazed, focus locked, a hint of sadness in his voice.

"Thanks for looking after me. Love you," he murmured.

Drawn to him, I leaned down. His lips tasted of wine, his clothes carried the faint trace of smoke, and beneath it all was the scent that was distinctly his. For a moment, I wanted to stay beside him and let the party carry on without us.

"I love you, too," I whispered, and I meant it.

Instead, I gave his hand a gentle squeeze, switched off the light, and stepped back into the noise of the party with the face I showed the world. No one would've suspected the tenderness that had passed behind that closed door.

That photo from the night still sits in my lounge room. Dave is in the middle, his arm around me. Joe is on the far end, both of them caught in the moment, laughing. And me, right there beside them, raising my eyebrows with that classic mum look that said: *What are you two up to now?*

Between them, I was happy.

Between them, I was loved.

Through everything that's happened, I know those two men would have done anything for me, each in their own way.

Now, as I sit here approaching sixty, I carry the weight of their absence. Dave never reached this milestone. Joe passed at sixty-one (61). Their loss makes this birthday feel less like a celebration and more like a reminder of what's gone.

If someone had told me that night that, nine years later, both of them would be gone, I wouldn't have believed it. Or I might've lashed out. But now I live that truth.

That night has stayed with me, and always will. It was one of those rare times when everything just felt right.

Some of my dearest friends. Joe's 60th, my 50th Serpentine 2016.

Joe (60), Dave, and me (50) celebrating our birthdays, 2016, Serpentine WA.

Chapter 11

Love Languages

I've only recently learned about the concept of love languages – odd, considering how much of my life I've spent trying to make sense of love in all its forms.

Apparently, there are five, and none of them involve sarcasm, passive-aggressive cleaning, or mysteriously disappearing when it's time to talk.

The idea is that we all give and receive love in different ways: words, actions, time, gifts, and touch. It's a whole theory.

Back then, the boys and I had no idea we were speaking languages. We were just doing our best, fumbling through an afternoon with whatever tools we had. A cold beer brought down to the shed, a fixed sink, a half-mumbled, "You right?"

That somehow said everything.

Now that I understand love languages, I can see how they were scattered throughout our relationships in very real ways.

Love, for me, has always been about connection, real, tangible connection. I don't just show love through words or gifts. I show it in the things I do. Acts of service have always been my natural love language. I cook, I nurture, I make life easier and happier for the people I love.

But when it comes to how I need love? That's different. I need to feel wanted, seen, and chosen, not just assumed, but actively acknowledged. I need words of encouragement, written or spoken. I need physical touch, hugs that wrap me up, a hand to hold, kisses, a thousand a day if possible. I need communication, not just the everyday kind, but the deep, meaningful kind.

It might sound like a contradiction, because if I were to describe myself, I'd say I was fiercely independent, bossy even.

But maybe that's why it worked with Dave. We shared similar needs, both of us driven by a longing for connection and reassurance. And in his own way, he gave me that.

He let me boss him around, not in a mean way, but in the small, caring ways that showed I was watching out for him.

"Have you eaten?"

"Have you taken your medication?"

"You shouldn't be smoking."

"Have you had a shower?"

He would never admit it, but I knew he liked the constant concern. Though if you'd asked him, he probably would've called it constant nagging.

There you go, who knew nagging could be a love language?

Dave used to say, "I don't know what you see in someone like me. I'm just an old bloke with nothing to offer."

I'd look straight at him and say, "You offer me peace. You're kind. You make me feel safe. And I think you're very handsome, too."

He'd grin and shrug it off with, "You're just saying that."

And I'd shrug right back: "Well, I don't always get what you see in me either. Maybe that's the point."

We were both people who needed to hear it; words of affirmation mattered to us. Maybe that's what made it work. We were a bit unsure of ourselves, but we were sure of each other.

Physical touch was a big one for Dave, not just the intimate stuff, but the everyday kind. A quick hug, legs touching, his hand on my knee while we watched telly. He liked being close.

And he loved a back scratch. Always had. Even as a kid, apparently. When his nieces and nephews were little, they'd take turns scratching his back like it was part of some Uncle David contract.

I didn't love it, got bored too quickly, and I hated that Deep Heat stuff. It'd stick to my hands and stink for hours. But if he'd had a rough day, I'd give in, scratch his back and rub in the Deep Heat for ten minutes, tops. He'd lie on the lounge room floor like a big kid, chin in his hands, and say, "Just five more minutes? Please?"

I'd roll my eyes, but I'd do it. Then, once I was done, I'd flop down and say, "My turn!"

And to be fair, he always returned the favour, proper massage, shoulders, the lot. He definitely gave better than he got.

We didn't know it, but we were practically love language experts by then.

When it came to acts of service, Dave appreciated them, up to a point. He'd come out of the bedroom with a half-grumble: "Hey, where's my flannel shirt?"

"I washed it," I'd reply.

"I only had it on for five minutes. It wasn't even dirty."

"It smelled like smoke," I'd shoot back.

He'd roll his eyes and sigh. "You don't have to wash everything every day. You're starting to remind me of my mum."

"Maybe that was her love language," I'd tease.

He'd shake his head, not even knowing what I meant, and with his voice full of cheek, say, "So … do I have a shirt I'm allowed to wear that you reckon is clean enough?"

Love wasn't always about what we did for each other; it was in the way we spoke, the way we reassured, and the way we kept things light when life felt heavy.

If I was frustrated or doubting myself, Dave would try to make me laugh. I'd be in the bathroom getting dressed, yelling out in frustration, "Nothing fits! I've got nothing to wear!"

He'd be out in the lounge trying to watch TV, and without missing a beat, he'd yell back, "With all those dresses jammed into my wardrobe and all that shopping you do, you can't find one thing to wear?"

I'd pull a face in the mirror, mimicking him silently. Then, his tone would soften.

"Doesn't matter what you wear. You're beautiful just the way you are."

That small exchange, banter, reassurance, a shared moment across the hallway, was our love language.

I'd smile to myself, even if he couldn't see it. His kindness was a mix of humour and affection. It always knew where to land.

Everyday life with Dave was full of those little gestures. I'd walk in from work and he'd be standing there, proud as anything.

"Did the washing," he'd say casually. "Separated the darks from the lights and even did the towels by themselves, like you said."

I'd laugh, put on my best over-the-top voice and say, "Oh my gosh, Dave, I'm so proud of you. Thank you so much."

He'd light up every time. He wanted to feel useful. To still show up.

Then, still grinning: "Got your cuppa tea ready, want one?"

"Yes, please. You know you make the best househusband."

And he did.

Joe.

Where do I even start with this guy?

A heart as big as Phar Lap and just as ruthless as The Godfather.

Of course, Joe loved physical touch, hugs from his family, a blanket tucked around him when he settled in for the night. He could be a bit of a softie when he wanted to be.

But his main love language?

Gift-giving.

He built me a house. Never said sorry, not once, but he'd turn up with a brand-new car or something special after a fight.

There was this time I was so mad at him I could've thrown the teapot straight at his head, but it was Royal Albert, the exact one I'd pointed out at the shops weeks earlier, the one I said I loved.

We'd had a silly argument where he'd said, "When Mum passes, you can have one of hers."

Like that was supposed to be romantic.

I didn't want to inherit something someday. I wanted to feel seen, loved, right now.

So when he turned up with that teapot, I knew. That was his version of, "I'm sorry, love."

I never threw it. I treasured it instead.

He had a way of wrapping up his feelings in presents. Cars I didn't need, presents that came wrapped in gold paper and beautiful bows, jewellery that was precious and always thoughtfully picked.

Looking back, I think gift-giving was more than just Joe's love language; it came from something deeper.

He never let go of the bike story. His little brother got a brand-new one for his birthday; Joe got a secondhand one a few weeks later. He carried that hurt.

Same with watches. He'd always wanted one as a kid and never got it. As an adult, he made up for it; he wore the flashiest ones and kept tins full of them tucked away in the cupboard.

So when our kids wanted something special, especially a bike or a watch, they got the best. He'd missed out growing up, and maybe this was his way of making sure no one else ever felt the way he did.

So for my 50th? He'd given in to my pleas to get me a Mercedes convertible. I'd longed for that for years, but as my birthday approached and our 20th wedding anniversary, I asked, "Could we trade it for a trip to Europe?"

He hesitated for just a second, then nodded. "If you want, let me know what's going on."

He wasn't much help planning, barely acting interested. At one point, I snapped, "I might as well go by myself. You don't have to come if you don't want to."

He looked at me, voice sharp. "Who else is gonna bloody look after you?"

That was Joe-speak for I love you.

So off we went.

Castles in Scotland, statues of poets in Ireland, gardens at the Chelsea Flower Show.

At Edinburgh Castle, I stood in a room where queens had feasted and birthed babies and kings had ruled entire kingdoms. No novel, no movie, no words could have captured the feeling I had that day. An act of love by Joe that I'll always be thankful for.

In London, I wandered through Harrods, touching silks and buying gifts. Joe waited outside, happy to sit in a café reading the paper. I'd duck in and out, dropping bags at his feet.

As I went to wander off again, he'd yell out, "Enjoy yourself, love. Make sure you spend all the money."

That was code for I love you, too.

In return, Joe liked a "good wife", one who did all the right things – cooked, cleaned, and spoke politely in front of the people he considered important.

He liked the finer things in life, especially when he wanted to be on show: crisp shirts, expensive cologne, and designer sunglasses. And he liked me to make sure they were all ready and waiting when he needed them.

When things were good, I used to like doing it. I'd try to explain to him that I cooked dinner every night, not because I had to, but because I wanted to. It was an act of service, my way of showing love.

But love wasn't always about European holidays. Diamond rings and a clean kitchen, sometimes it looked like turning up to a place you would rather not set foot in.

One afternoon, Joe was out making Italian sausages at an old friend's place. I'd driven over with a carton of beers he wanted. As I climbed out of the car, I was cautious; the dogs were feral, rubbish was everywhere, and the place was a food safety disaster. I wouldn't have touched that salami if you paid me.

When I handed him the beers, he reached out. One of his big, hard-working hands came toward my face, smelling faintly of pork and fennel. He gently wiped something, dirt, maybe, from my forehead.

For a second, I was taken aback. That tiny gesture was so unlike him. In that moment, he saw me. I mattered.

I've remembered it all these years later, because there was a gentle tenderness that wasn't often shown in this hard, complicated man

Another time, my car battery died. I called Joe. He was nearby, so he drove out to where I was.

I told him, "You don't have to wait. The RAC's on the way."

He leaned against the bonnet and said, "I'm not leaving you here by yourself."

I asked again, surprised. This was the man who could vanish for two weeks, no calls, no explanation.

But there he was, watching the sun go down in the car park, refusing to leave my side.

That's the thing about Joe. He didn't say the words much. So I'd tuck them away, like treasures in a drawer.

Sometimes, love isn't loud.

It's a Royal Albert teapot instead of an apology.

It's a hand reaching for your face when you don't expect it.

It's someone staying beside you when you've already told them they don't have to.

And that's more than enough.

If I'd sat either of them down, Joe or Dave, and started talking about "love languages," they would've rolled their eyes, shaken their heads, and grinned at each other like, "What's she on about now?"

But the truth is, they both spoke them. All five.

They just didn't know it had a name.

And that was the most beautiful part of all.

Chapter 12

Housesitting

It didn't matter whose house it was; if we were there together, it felt like home.

House-sitting for family and friends gave us that: time to just be together, without interruption.

We slept in their spare rooms, filled their fridges, and cooked dinner in their kitchens. For a little while, we pretended it was our life.

In every place we stayed, I noticed the little things: the scent of their air freshener, family photos frozen in time on the walls, a book left behind on the coffee table. Those homely touches didn't just help us settle in; they gave us a sense of belonging.

Dave was the kind of guy you trusted without a second thought. Once you got to know him, you truly saw who he was.

So when his mum went off to Scotland for months at a time, it was always Dave she trusted to look after the house. Same with Sue, one of his mum's oldest friends and a steady advocate for Dave. She'd always fill the bar fridge with treats and drinks as a little thank you for him looking after her thriving pot plants and keeping everything secure.

For us, it felt normal, even if, by most standards, it probably wasn't. I'd go shopping, stock up for our stay, then head home to take care of things there. It was a strange arrangement, but it worked.

Some nights I stayed, others I couldn't. I'd come in, drop the bags on the counter.

"Got your favourites," I'd say, while Dave put the kettle on. We'd settle in like we owned the place. Dinner out under the patio, the scent of Sue's flowers in the air. Or on the couch watching TV, side by side. I think we watched all of Peaky Blinders there, like it was the most natural thing in the world.

Dave loved house-sitting his mum's place, especially in the colder months when his parents went off for the Scottish summer. The gas fire was always on, casting a warm glow as we lay in front of it. He'd stretch out, arms behind his head, and say, "I used to lie like this when I was a kid, talking to Mum, watching TV with her while the old man was away."

I'd smile at him, enjoying the glimpse of his past. I liked to see him happy.

He tried to be romantic once, placing candles on the hearth – but the wax dripped onto the carpet.

"I'm gonna get in trouble for this," he said, half-laughing.

I told him to put the brown paper down and iron it.

But when I came back the next day, the wax was still there, and now the carpet was burnt.

"What happened?" I asked.

"I ironed it ... Forgot the brown paper."

Just another unintentional misdemeanour by Dave.

If I were at home, I'd get my daughter off to school, take care of what I needed to, then head over to Dave's.

He always slept in, so I'd knock gently. A few moments later, the door would creak open, and there he'd be, half-dressed, eyes heavy with sleep, warmth radiating off him like the house itself.

I'd slip out of being Mum, the worker, the housekeeper, and into something softer. Just for me.

With Dave, I became a different version of myself, someone who got to have quiet mornings, warm arms, and comfort. I'd step inside and wrap my arms around him, pressing my face into his chest.

"I can feel the love coming out of your body just by hugging you," I'd whisper.

"Come back to bed," he'd mumble, pulling me in, and I always would.

We'd curl up under the blankets, talking in that half-awake, dreamlike way. Sometimes, we'd doze off again, waking up warm and content, stretching lazily before finally getting up.

The rest of the day would unfold in quiet, familiar ways. We'd make tea, maybe toast. He'd lean against the counter while I pottered around the kitchen, chatting about whatever came to mind, how the car was running, what the traffic was like on the school run, whether we needed more bread. We didn't say much that was important, but the conversation never stopped. It was easy. Comfortable. Like any other couple in any other kitchen.

Then he'd go quiet for a second, looking out the window like he was memorising the already-familiar view.

"I wish we lived here," he'd say.

I knew it wasn't just the house; it was what it held for him: the memories of his mum, the comfort of something steady. Back then, it was all just a dream, one we weren't sure would ever come true.

Once, he looked at me and said, "Living here with you, that would be my dream come true."

He said it with a lopsided smile, like he was only half-serious. But I knew him well enough by then to understand what was underneath it. Sometimes he said things that way, half-joking, because he wasn't sure how I'd respond. I heard the sincerity in it. I always did. That vulnerability.

And the thing was, it was a dream for me, too. Maybe not in that house, but one day, to live in a home with him.

And eventually, we did. We got our place. It just didn't last as long as we'd hoped.

And when the house-sitting ended, when they came home, we packed our belongings. We wiped down benches, swept floors, made beds, and disappeared back to our own homes, back to our realities.

Until the next house-sit came along, and we could pretend all over again.

Borrowed spaces. Borrowed time.

That was our reality.

Chapter 13

My Favourite Italian

I've shared everything I can about Joe, the good times, the challenges, and the heartbreak. Now, as I say goodbye, I feel a mix of gratitude and sadness. This farewell is a chance for me to reflect on everything he brought into my life. I can still hear his laughter and feel his warm hugs. Saying goodbye means I have to let him go, but it also means holding onto our memories and cherishing the love we shared. It's about not letting past hurts get in the way of new beginnings.

My Italian wasn't the kind from a postcard or a pasta ad; mine was loud, proud, maddening. He could charm a room and ruin a day in the same breath. But he was mine. And if you'd met him, really met him, you'd remember. Sometimes he'd start off speaking in English, then switch to broken English, and before you knew it, he'd be full-on Italian, waving his hands around like a conductor. If you didn't know better, you'd think he was yelling. But that was Joe's way of communicating, passionately expressing every thought and feeling.

And now, as I navigate this sea of grief, for everything I shared and lost with Joe, I can finally admit there was an undeniable, deep love between us. Complicated, yes. But still love.

When things were good, and Joe was working away, I often felt a spark of joy as I picked him up from the airport. I'd settled into a hopeful mindset, believing this time would be different.

Those first 24 hours were always the best. I'd see him coming down the escalator, bag in one hand, scanning the crowd until he spotted me. He'd wrap me in a big bear hug, and in those moments, there was a light in him, proud, warm, reminding me why I loved him.

On the way home from the airport, he happily talked about how our son and his family were doing up there. When we walked in the door, he'd see his daughter and say, "Hey, Weenie?" His genuine delight was contagious. Our other daughter would wander over and say, "Papa," and he'd laugh that silly, half-snorted laugh that didn't quite match his big frame. I'd look at him and think, *I love you*. I always loved seeing that version of him, even if it was short-lived.

It was moments like these that reminded me of his strength, even during the tough times, like when I remember the building supervisor giving me a hard time when we were building our new home. I called Joe at work, and he came straight home, fuming. As he walked across the gravel, heavy work boots crunching with each step, dark eyes blazing, the supervisor's smug and cocky attitude instantly changed. He put his hands up and said, "I don't want any trouble, mate."

At that moment, I felt a rush of pride, not because he was angry, but because he showed up for me. That was Joe, my fiery, forceful Italian.

Over the years, I'm sure Joe and I caused our children more heartache and confusion than we ever meant to. It was never our intention. We loved you all so very much, even when life around us was messy and uncertain.

I hope you remember the good times too, the freedom of growing up on the farm, running up rows of beans, eating fresh fruit straight from the tree, and tearing through the paddocks on motorbikes, the wind in your hair and the sun on your faces. Laughter echoing through the yard, the smell of cut grass, the sound of sprinklers, and the days spent in the pool until your fingers wrinkled.

Joe shared his culture with you – from growing food and making Italian sausages to bottling tomato sauce and keeping the old wine barrel in the shed. In his own quiet way, he showed the value of hard work and pride in what you create. Through all of Joe's faults, he loved you deeply, and through all of mine, I loved you even more.

Our marriage is hard to explain, like a storm that never quite passed. One minute, I was overwhelmed by everything around me, and the next, I'd find myself smiling as I walked into our home, the rich aroma of his spaghetti and meatballs simmering on the stove. And there he stood, the kitchen a complete disaster. I'd reach up and kiss him, his familiar moustache tickling my face. The delicious scent filled the room, and in that moment, the richness of our lives together reminded me that there was still joy.

One of my fondest family memories is of Joe dancing around the living room with our daughter, watching *Dancing with the Stars*. He was always her willing partner, spinning and laughing, his size-twelve feet clunking against the floor in time with her tiny ones. To her, he was always her champion, her first true love.

He carried this tenderness for the kids wherever he went, scooping up our granddaughters as they ran to him, calling out, "Poppy!" He held them like they were the most precious treasures in the world.

Joe loved his routine, too. Every morning, he'd pick up the Western Australian newspaper, a habit that became a running joke in our family. "Can someone get me the paper?" he'd ask, and there'd be groans all around. Even the kids would roll their eyes and say, "Where's Dad? Oh, gone to get the paper?"

Beneath the humour lay an infamous truth; often, it was a thinly veiled excuse to indulge in his vices. When he passed, we memorialised this quirky habit by placing a piece of poly pipe on his headstone, inscribed with: "The Paper." And we remember him fondly.

We held each other less than we should have, looking for love elsewhere. But even then, there was something between us, undeniable, and real.

When it mattered most, I turned back. I showed up. Every time he got sick, I was there, holding his hand, steadying his body. I can still feel the weight of his hard-working hands in mine, weathered from years spent toiling the earth. His gold wedding band still graced his finger, a reminder of our vows.

The Car.

Joe had been missing all day. We couldn't get hold of him, not unusual, but something didn't sit right with my daughter and me. As the day went on, my daughter decided to try and track his phone. She did, and we drove there, slightly panicked but trying not to let it show.

We found him in the car. The engine was still running. His head was slumped forward.

I ripped the door open and turned off the ignition. He'd been sitting in the car for so long.

I pulled his head back like they show you in first aid courses, and I heard him gasp. He was breathing.

"Run, love. Go to the shop and find out the address, call an ambulance."

I rang Dave and my eldest daughter and told them what had happened. He and his sister Elaine drove straight down, as did my daughter. They were all there beside me the whole time. It was touch and go, but we had found him. He was still ours.

After the incident, Joe suffered a hypoxic brain injury. It affected his memory and the way his body and mind worked, changing everything about how he functioned day to day.

The Final Days.

When Joe lost all capability, when he couldn't talk, walk, or even eat, we never stopped trying. We sat with him for hours, talking to him, showing him pictures, doing everything we could to pull him back to us. And then, it was like a miracle. Joe came back; he spoke again, slowly learned to write, did his physio, walked, showered, and laughed. But his short-term memory was gone. He knew who we were, but couldn't remember the small things, where the cups were, where our bedroom was. We labelled the doors. We made it work. We carried on, together.

The next six months were exhausting. And then came the news we hadn't known was hiding: Joe had renal cancer. His heart, already under strain, couldn't take the pressure.

We didn't have time to fall apart – hospitals, doctor's visits, and finding out every option we had.

When Joe came home, the nights were worse for him. He couldn't settle. He'd get confused, worried. I'd sit beside him, dozing on the lounge, the drone of the TV in the background.

Every movement he made would startle me awake.

"Are you okay, love? What's wrong?"

One night, he decided he was going to look for something to eat at three o'clock in the morning. I got up and followed him into the kitchen, dragging myself with a weariness that made it hard to even put one foot in front of the other. Still, I kept my voice soft, patient.

"What do you fancy, love?"

Moments like that became the rhythm of our days. Gentle, draining, full of love and sadness.

That night, the morphine drip relieved Joe's suffering, yet he stirred. He reached out, hands lifting toward me, trying to sit up. I gently placed my hands on his chest, encouraging him to lie back down. He sank into the chair, and I felt the ache of hopelessness wash over me like a wave. I wanted to fix it. I wanted to do something. I wanted to change the ending, but I knew there was nothing I could do but whisper words of comfort.

"It's okay, love. Just rest now."

For years after, I've wondered ... was he trying to say something? Did I take away his last words? Did I miss his final message? Those questions haunt me still.

Until recently, I read somewhere that people often reach out to loved ones in heaven when they're passing. I like to think now that Joe was reaching out to his mum. No matter how old he was, he was still her son, and that gives me peace.

I always imagined death as something almost holy, angels descending, soft music, a peaceful slipping away. But Joe's final breath was jagged, desperate.

I leaned close, whispering softly, It's okay, Joe. I'm right here. You can rest now. I wanted him to feel safe, to know he wasn't alone. But in my heart, I was pleading, *Please don't go. We won't be able to survive this without you.* His breath was jagged, uneven. And then ... his chest was still.

The room seemed to freeze. For a moment, nothing moved, nothing breathed.

My daughter's cry came then, so raw, so profound. It filled the room, a sound pulled from the deepest part of her, the ache of someone breaking.

And then the nurse's voice, clear and real: "Time of death, twelve fifteen."

And just like that, my favourite Italian was gone. Our family would never be the same again.

In the days that followed, I was a shadow of myself. I curled into bed or sat for hours in the chair where he'd passed, barely able to function. I moved his chair into my room – the very chair where he took his last breath. It felt like an impossible task as I dragged it through the doorway. I couldn't give up; it was where it needed to be. If I sat in it, maybe I could smell his scent lingering in the fabric, bringing his soul closer to me as I felt his arms embrace me, strong and sure. I remember numbly watching Grace and Frankie on Netflix for hours, just to escape the relentless ache in my chest.

If it hadn't been for my daughter-in-law, cooking, tending the house, holding us all together, I don't know what would have happened.

Joe wasn't a practising Catholic, but tradition mattered to him. We honoured his wishes with a rosary, a church service, and the Lord's Prayer in both English and Italian. He looked at peace in his favourite leather jacket. The boys wore black suits with red ties, Joe's favourite colour. At the graveside, we released 99 red balloons and placed 99 red carnations, his mother's favourite flower, and his favourite number was 9. No expense was spared. I wanted the best for him.

I remember standing there, terrified the pallbearers might drop his coffin. I remember the wake afterwards, though truthfully, it's a blur.

What I remember most is turning to my son and saying, "Take me home. I just want to go home."

I remember standing at the gate when I got the death certificate. It was something I'd dreaded. I'm not even sure why – maybe because it made everything feel so final.

As I opened it, the word 'untreated' caught my eye instantly.

It ripped something in me.

I stood there sobbing, calling it out like a question, 'Untreated?'

To the birds.

To the trees.

To Joe, wherever he was.

We didn't turn our backs. We didn't walk away. We did everything we could. But there was no curing it. His memory was already almost gone. He would've been terrified by chemo, by hospitals, by strangers poking and prodding.

We chose peace. We chose home.

How is that untreated?

We treated him with gentleness, with love, with soft voices and familiar faces. With warm blankets and favourite meals, songs and music he knew.

His heart wouldn't have made it through treatment, but we made it through with him.

And when the time came, all Joe wanted was to be home. Not lost in a hospital. Just home, with us.

And they dare to write 'untreated', as if we didn't love him enough to fight.

Joe's passing left an enduring void in the lives of his children and me, leaving our hearts to ache with the pain of his absence. Despite his struggles, we loved him immensely.

Joe's death didn't just leave a gap in our home; it left a gap in our souls. Grief softened with time, but it never vanished.

Love like that leaves an imprint, one you learn to live with, but never fully forget. Joe is with me always, even when new relationships begin.

His photos have always hung on the walls; they always will. I see him smile at me from them. How can I ever eat spaghetti without thinking of him?

He is part of our family, our culture, and some of those traditions will continue for a lifetime, not only for me, but my children, and their children.

He will be spoken of often. He was a larger-than-life man, and men like that aren't easily forgotten.

Goodbye Joe. I love you always xx.

Me and Joe, 2017, Princess Cruise at the British Isles.

Chapter 14

No Fuss, Just Us

People pretend not to judge, but they do. Some don't even bother pretending. A few say it outright.

"Is she seeing Dave now?"

They whisper it like gossip, as if they knew him, as if they knew me.

It reminds me of how widows were treated in the early 1900s. You were expected to mourn for a year, sometimes longer. Unless you were poor or had mouths to feed, then it was called survival. We're meant to be more modern now, but those old ideas linger, not as rules, but as comments, raised eyebrows, quiet judgment when you mention a "new friend."

It's different for men. When they find someone new, people say: "Good for him. He needs someone."

But for women? You're rushed. Cold. Disrespectful. Like you've done something wrong just for trying to feel happy again.

But aren't I allowed to feel the warmth of someone's hand in mine? To laugh over coffee on a cold winter's day, sitting close in a cafe booth, just glad to have company? To want comfort, safety, and something to look forward to? It's not about replacing anyone. It's not about forgetting. Joe will always be a part of me. But I'm still here, me, figuring it out, one day at a time.

When Dave and I went away for the weekend, there was a lightness, a happiness, and yes, a little doubt too. That quiet voice still asked what people might think. Thirteen months later, it lingered.

Of course, we were heading to an AC/DC event. Anyone who knew Dave knew he was a die-hard fan. Whenever the band came to Perth or there was a tribute, even a knockoff band, we'd go. But this one felt different. It was the first time we went out in public together since Joe passed.

Dave had an extensive collection of AC/DC memorabilia, books, records, CDs, and t-shirts. If they made it, he had it. His love for music was part of who he was. He knew every lyric to every song. He could rattle off facts about the band and its members like he'd lived it himself.

So when we heard about the Highway to Hell event, there was no question. We booked a little B&B in Fremantle to attend the 40th anniversary of Bon Scott's death on March 1, 2020. Joe had been gone a year. This felt like the right moment, an opportunity for us to just be.

They closed off a ten-kilometre stretch of Canning Highway, the road Bon Scott often travelled to reach his favourite pub – *The Raffles Hotel*. Its steep descent near the pub made it notorious for crashes, earning the nickname Highway to Hell.

We spent the afternoon in the crowd, soaking up the energy, and ducked into a pub for a few drinks. Dave had slowed down a bit over the years, but this was Bon Scott. He was celebrating, full rock'n'roll style.

He nearly got into a fight with some young bloke who gave me a sideways glance and a smart remark.

Dave looked at me. I caught his eye and gave him that look that said, "Don't spoil the night."

So he let it go. Sometimes he forgot his age. He still thought he was ten feet tall and bulletproof.

The atmosphere was electric. We stood for hours, waiting for the trucks to roll past, each carrying a different band belting out AC/DC songs. Music echoed through the street. Everywhere you looked, there were flannel shirts, cut-off shorts, band tees, and devil's horns, which I proudly wore.

The bands couldn't quite fill AC/DC's shoes. Dave made his disappointment loud enough for everyone to hear.

We were both starting to tire. There was a slight stagger to his step. We'd been jumping up and down all afternoon, walking long stretches of the highway. We weren't over it, just ready to leave the noise behind and step into the quiet.

After hours of music and movement, the stillness of the B&B felt like a sanctuary.

It was a redone 1900s cottage with modern comforts. We took advantage of the space and privacy. Long showers, complimentary chocolate, soft lighting … something shifted. Maybe it was the atmosphere. Maybe the drinks. Maybe just the timing.

The way Dave looked at me that night felt different. It was probably the booze and I do tend to read into things, but it felt more than just physical. There was this unexpected sense of us. After years of secrecy, I'd forgotten what it felt like to be free.

I won't go into all the details; my kids, his nieces and nephews, and our grandkids don't need a play-by-play of a romantic night between two old, grown adults. But I'll say this: no matter how old you are, you're still capable of deep, passionate love, of wanting to be seen, held, and wanted.

And we did. We wanted each other. We loved each other.

It wasn't just physical. It was tender, meaningful, wrapped in care and connection, and everything we'd carried to that moment. To feel that kind of closeness again meant something.

We weren't two people grieving or hiding a relationship anymore.

We were just Brigitte and Dave.

The next morning, I was still snuggled up in that big, luxurious bed. Slow starts were a luxury in themselves. I glanced over at him in the kitchen, barefoot, bare-chested, making coffee. Soft morning light spilled through the window and caught the shape of him, the curve of his shaved head, that AC/DC tattoo proudly on display.

My love for him at that moment was almost too much to put into words. So deep. So full. It caught in my throat.

I thought about saying something about the night before, the tenderness, the passion, but would it make things awkward?

I always got embarrassed about that sort of stuff.

Not Dave. He never got embarrassed about anything.

I hesitated. Then I just blurted it out: "So, what do you reckon about last night?"

He gave me a little grin. "Yeah, good. How about you?"

"Yeah," I said, trying not to smile.

That was it. No big speeches. No deep conversations. Just a quiet knowing. We were on the same page.

He stirred his coffee and asked, "So what's the plan? I know you love a plan."

I laughed. I did love a plan. And of course, I had one: a walk along the river, coffee at the Dome, pretty standard for us by then.

But something about that morning felt like a beginning. Just us. No fuss.

And for the first time in a long time, that was more than enough.

Chapter 15

An Isolated Incident

There was more to Dave than people knew. On the outside, he played the jokester, always quick with a laugh or a smart comment. He could make people smile, even when he was hiding his own pain.

What most didn't see was how much he carried inside: the frustrations, the lack of confidence, and the way being misunderstood ate away at him.

"I'm not stupid, you know. People think I'm just a dumb cunt," he'd say. Though blunt, his words concealed an ache to be seen beyond the surface.

Dave's intelligence was subtle and often overlooked. People judged him too quickly, but beneath that rough exterior lay a deeply compassionate heart and an inquisitive mind, always eager to learn and grow. He could rattle off more facts about history and music than most. When it came to machinery, he had a knack for dismantling engines, fixing appliances, and repairing gardening equipment I would have tossed aside. Yet despite these skills, his speech was often hesitant, and his struggle to articulate himself betrayed the depth of his thoughts. Each dismissive glance or patronising remark cut deeper than he ever let on.

Behind all that humour and ability was also depression. Suicide carried a heavy stigma in our era. Mental health issues weren't talked about, and men were often left to face their struggles alone. Dave only ever spoke about trying to take his own life in fragments, cryptic comments that never went too deep.

The scars on his stomach told part of the story. When doctors asked, he'd shrug and say, "Bowel surgery," and that was that. I knew the truth. He came to me in his own time and talked about what he wanted to, but I knew better than to push. Some wounds aren't meant to be reopened, and some stories come out only when they're ready.

I think his suicidal thoughts came from a desperate need to be seen, not from a simple wish to die. He'd snap things out in a rush.

What do people see in me? Do they think they can take the piss all the time? Do they think I'm just a druggie, nothing more?"

And then get frustrated because the words wouldn't come out right. He couldn't explain what he felt, and the effort of trying to say it, and failing, chipped away at his self-worth until it felt like too much to bear. I'd tell him, "I understand, Dave," over and over, and that seemed to help. All he needed was to hear, "I hear you. I believe in you."

I saw the other side of him. When I encouraged him, asked about the things he knew, or praised him for fixing what I would have thrown away, I'd see him smile from the inside out. Being seen and valued brought out his gentleness, his humour, his love. Those were the moments when his true heart came through so clearly.

And maybe that's why I understood him so well. I'd walked close to that same edge myself, and I knew how heavy those thoughts could be. He struggled with words, but in those moments of encouragement, he found simple ways to show me his love.

I've still got a card he gave me once. Inside, in his messy scrawl, it says, "You know I'm not very good with words, so you'll just have to imagine how much I love you." It wasn't intellectual. Just simple. Just him.

Even now when I take that card out of the drawer, the card is starting to wear with age. I can almost hear his voice in that messy scrawl. It's proof of what he couldn't always say out loud. I hope he knows how much comfort those words give me today.

When he said things like, "It'd be easier to die," I could feel the weight of his despair, see it in the way his shoulders slumped, an admission of defeat and an expression of how overwhelmed he felt.

Have you ever felt that despair, not knowing where to turn?

He didn't know how to ask for the help he desperately needed. Instead, it spiralled. Sometimes it showed up in reckless drug and alcohol use; other times, it came out in violent outbursts. His sister once snapped at him, "If you say that again, you won't need to kill yourself, I'll do it for you!" She meant well, tough love and all. To me, it sounded more like frustration than anything, but that was how she dealt with him.

Once, driving through the bush, he pointed out the window and said, "I tried to kill myself up there once."

I froze.

"Oh my god, what did you do?"

"Drank a whole bottle of Scotch. Didn't work," he said, smiling slightly.

"A whole bottle?"

"Yeah, a litre bottle. Took some pills with it too."

I stared at him, shocked.

"I'm glad it didn't work," I said quietly. "Or you wouldn't be here with me now."

"Yeah … I'm glad too," he murmured with a faint smile.

I smiled back, but inside I felt sick. His story was a reminder that if things had gone differently, I might never have had him by my side in that moment.

Honestly, I was thankful for his crazy high tolerance for alcohol and drugs. It might've just saved his life that day.

There was another time he tried to take his own life, something I felt was a more serious attempt. An isolated incident, far away from everything. I wasn't there, so I only know bits and pieces of what he told me. He spoke about it rarely, but I could see the sadness in him when he did.

It happened at a remote roadhouse, halfway between Carnarvon and Kalbarri, surrounded by red dirt, rugged beauty, and the kind of silence that gets into your bones. On the surface, it looked peaceful. But inside? It had turned bleak.

We passed through once on a road trip. The sun was glaring, and dust swirled around the van as we pulled in. Dave glanced toward the building where he used to live.

"Shall we go in? Just have a drink at the bar?" I asked.

He looked at me and said quietly, "I'd rather not. Fuck 'em. It's something I'd rather forget."

I didn't ask who "them" meant. I could tell he didn't want to talk about it. He'd been banned from that bar, but the same people who kicked him out still gathered there every night. Surrounded by people, but completely alone. He told the story offhand, like it didn't matter anymore, but I could still hear the bitterness in his voice.

There was one thing that gave him comfort back then: a little goat. It followed him everywhere, hooves clicking over the red dirt, like his own shadow. Dave had a soft spot for animals, and he said he loved that little goat.

Then one day, his so-called mates killed it while he was away, cooked it on the barbecue, and told him straight out that it was his pet. They laughed about it in front of him.

The harsh reality is that some people can be unbelievably cruel. It makes you wonder: do people ever stop and think about the damage their words and actions cause? He didn't say much about it, only that he walked away with his fists clenched. I think that was a turning point. Maybe that's why he started talking about darker things, about the Samurai.

He once told me that in Japanese culture, it was more honourable to die by your own hand than to fall into enemy hands. That idea made sense to him then. The loneliness. The betrayals. The grief. It all added up to that moment. He never gave me the full story, only flickers here and there, but it was enough to piece together the image of a man drowning under the weight of it all.

Still, he survived. There was no big comeback. He just kept putting one foot in front of the other, and somehow that was enough.

He moved on to Carnarvon after that, and for a while, there were happier times. He found sunshine, work, and friends, a new routine in his life.

That chapter came to an end when he asked Joe and me to drive up to Carnarvon with the truck as his partner wanted to leave. We stayed the night at their home, and the next morning, as they were packing the truck, getting ready to leave, I pulled him aside. I hated the thought of him being on his own.

"Don't stay here by yourself, Dave," I said.

"I'll be alright," he told me.

"Don't you feel sad?" I asked.

He just gave me a little shrug. "Well, what can you do? If she wants to leave, she wants to leave."

I carried that with me as we drove away. I felt sad for him, left behind, isolated.

Later, he moved back to Perth, drifting in and out of what seemed to be transactional relationships. And then, somehow, we found each other again. The rest is history. And I hope, with all my heart, that in the end he felt understood.

There are still days when things feel too heavy to carry, and I think of him. I remember that he once felt the same way, but he kept going. He may not have realised it, but every step he took gave me the gift of those years we shared. That was the gift, that he stayed. And that's what matters most.

Chapter 16

The Gardener

Dave couldn't walk past a garden bed without tending to something. We'd pull into his parents' driveway for a quick visit, and before I'd even unbuckled my seatbelt, he was out the door, hat on stretching his back and fumbling for a smoke. He'd stroll over to the roses lining the driveway, casually plucking a weed, or deadheading a bloom, as if it were second nature. Cigarette in hand, he'd inspect the plants like the avid gardener he was, then finally swagger up to the door. Inside, he always had something to say:

"You need to prune them back. You need to spray. They've got a black spot. They need more water."

It drove his stepfather mad, but his mum just nodded, "Yes, son, we'll get on to it."

But long before Serpentine and all the gardens we made together, there was the family farm, five acres in Baldivis once owned by Joe's parents, framed by a sagging cyclone fence and a long driveway that led down toward the house. To the left were the old market gardens, once full of vegetables but now abandoned, choked with waist-high weeds. On the right was a paddock that had held a horse, sheep, and even pigs over the years.

Closer to the house was the citrus orchard with its lemons, oranges, and the best mandarins I've ever eaten, juicy and sweet, the kind you still remember years later. Out the front stood the jacaranda, and every spring it turned into a sea of purple. That tree shaded birthday parties, baby showers, and family photos. It was our family tree. My granddaughter Mia even got it tattooed on her back, swing and all. That's how much it meant to our family.

And then there was the acre of lush grass, always a bone of contention. Joe liked to claim he kept it looking good, but really it was usually me or Dave on the mower, while Joe stood with his hands on his hips, dishing out orders.

"I'm the boss around here," he'd bark, and I'd shoot back, "Boss of what, Joe?"

And if anyone pushed him too far, he'd roar, "Get off the property!" stretching out his arm and stabbing his finger toward the gate. That was Joe's line, and if you knew him, you would've heard it more than once.

The farm had its soundtrack too. The old heavy-duty sprinkler, forever with a flat tyre, was dragged across the yard with effort. With the flick of the bore switch, it would rattle into life:

Tick tick tick tick… shhhhhh… arcs of water spraying over the grass.

Sometimes things went wrong, like when the bore pump broke down. One day Joe lifted the lid and there, coiled at the bottom, was a tiger snake. Joe reckoned Dave should go down anyway.

Dave was up for most things, but he drew the line at snakes. "I'm not bloody going down there," he said.

I looked at Joe and said, "He's not going down there. Why would you even say that? Anyway, lunch is ready."

That was a role that never changed. Me calling them in, them stomping up with dusty boots and grubby hands, ready to devour whatever I'd put on the table. Mine and Dave's relationship had unspoken rules, and though that's hard to explain, we both wanted to protect the bond we all shared with Joe. When Joe was home, Dave never came inside looking for anything other than lunch. We were mindful of that.

Still Joe got grumpy at times. The drugs did that to him. Joe was a good man, but Joe the addict was different. Some days, he yelled at Dave about everything. Dave just took it in his stride. Not like me. I always had to fire back with some smart comment, sometimes making things worse, sometimes making Joe laugh.

He'd often shake his head at me and say, "You bite like a headless chook." I still don't know what he meant by that, even today. I'd look at Dave and say, "I don't know how you put up with him yelling at you like that." He'd just shrug and say, "That's just Joe. If he's yelling at me, he's not yelling at you."

I suppose he had a point.

At the end of the day, Joe and Dave would sit out back, light up their cigarettes, crack open a Jack Daniels and laugh about the day. There was a camaraderie between them. That's who they were, two old mates. Sadly, you can't make old friends, and Joe and Dave were exactly that till the day he died.

When Joe passed, the garden was still something that had to be done, lawns to mow, weeds to pull, the usual jobs. But for Dave, it became more than that. What had once been work turned into something he enjoyed, something that gave him peace. We settled into it together, chatting as we planted or weeded. I always wore gloves, while he plunged his bare hands into the soil, fingernails full of dirt. Side by side.

Together we grew rows of capsicum, tomatoes and zucchini. Each morning we'd check on our veggie patch like kids, peering under leaves to see what had sprouted overnight.

Birds became part of everyday life. Cheeky Willy Wagtails danced across the lawn with their tails fanning. But it was the magpies that really claimed Dave. They waited for him each morning and again in the evening, calling out until he came to feed them titbits of mince. He'd sit out the front for hours, content in their company.

Lockdown in 2020 deepened that bond between us and the garden. One year, Dave gave us a peach tree for Christmas, and although the woman at the nursery said it would never fruit without a companion tree, it thrived. It produced so much that we learned to preserve the peaches. Rows of those jars were stacked in the pantry as if we were preparing for the end of the world, and to be honest, we thought we were.

Dave even built a chicken coop, while Leo the sulphur-crested cockatoo provided a running commentary from his perch, mimicking my voice perfectly with the shrill call of, "Davvve!" much to the amusement of visitors. In those strange months, our little oasis was our perfect sanctuary.

We marked ANZAC Day at the front gate, a lantern glowing made from an old milk bottle, a wreath fashioned of gum leaves hanging beside. During lockdown we got a bit crafty, making decorations and enjoying the simple act of doing things by hand. The bugle echoed through the trees, eerie and beautiful.

Afterwards, we cooked bacon and eggs in the garage, billy tea on the gas cooker, until the chill chased us back inside to the wood fire where we sat close, leaning into each other, embracing the warmth.

It was a time that shaped us. And it was during those months that Dave's reputation as "Dave the Gardener" grew when we opened a small café in town. He never wanted payment, just a banana thick shake, as he swept paths and pulled weeds. We would head up there in the evening as the sun set, wave to locals pushing prams, and watch the horses wander slowly past with their riders, the horses' tails swishing, blending into a perfectly peaceful evening. That was country living at its finest. The strip of dirt out front became a thriving garden under his care, and though it's neglected now, a gum tree he planted still rises strong, a living reminder of him.

Evening watering Serpentine February 2022

Then there was Warnbro. I bought that place after Joe passed. The selling point for me was the garden out the back, big river rocks, and a solid limestone wall backing onto the main road. Dave got straight onto planting bougainvillea, rambling roses, anything with a prickly leaf on it. Added security, he said.

That garden holds a lot for me. Once, while repotting, I uncovered a little rock with our names scratched into it, mine, his, and my grandson's. Such an ordinary thing, but I pressed it to my cheek and felt him right there beside me. I'm thankful for that garden, because one day it will be my forever home, and I'll always have a little piece of Dave there.

From big backyards to small spaces, each garden told its own story. His unit was no different. Dave's little place only had a balcony, but it became his oasis. At first, I gave him a couple of small plants, just something to keep him busy, a little morning routine. Before long the whole patio was covered in greenery. It turned into a peaceful little spot. I'd sit in the rocking chair at the little table, reading a book, while Dave fussed with the plants. I've got fond memories of that unit too.

We created gardens wherever we lived – Warnbro, Wellard, and Serpentine. Each space held cuttings from the last, pot plants dragged across towns and suburbs until, finally, in our own little unit, all those plants came together in one small courtyard. It was meant to be our first real home together, and for a few short months, it was. I already knew I had to leave Serpentine; it was too big to manage alone once Dave was gone. I needed his help to move and wanted the chance to create some memories with him in the new unit before he left.

At that stage, we were still in denial. We told ourselves we'd buy the unit, lock it up and travel, but deep down, we both knew the truth. Eventually, the reality settled in. What we really needed was a quiet place where Dave could hang up his hat and find peace and solitude at the end of his life.

Was that too much for any man to ask for? I don't think so.

Chapter 17

The Catch

Fishing was one of Dave's favourite pastimes. Like gardening, it brought him peace, open spaces, and the sense of being surrounded by nature instead of noise. The gentle sound of the water calmed him, especially when life felt heavy.

Whenever we travelled, his rods and that battered old tackle box were the first things in the van. I could buy him a brand-new rod, and I did, more than once, but within a week the tip would be snapped and the whole thing patched with black duct tape. He was always enthusiastic, casting it out like he was trying to lasso a whale. I'd shake my head and warn him to slow down when he packed, or he'd end up breaking something. Sure enough, he always did.

He was accident-prone in the most Dave kind of way: a hook through the finger one day, his walking stick slipping off the jetty the next. He was a good fisherman, but just as much a character. Sometimes he'd be out there, knee-deep in the water, determined to land the perfect catch, only to nick himself again.

"Careful, Dave," I'd call out. "You know sharks are attracted to blood; with all that dripping, it's a wonder there's not a school circling already."

He'd grin and say, "Well, there's not much of me left to eat now, is there?"

"Dave, don't say shit like that," I'd reply, half-laughing, half-serious.

Now and then, his rod would bend and his eyes would light up as he shouted, "This is a big one!"

I'd watch him reel it in, full of drama, until a small fish broke the surface, glimmering in the sun. He'd hold it up proudly and quip, "The dad must've got away." I couldn't help but laugh.

Still, he'd fish anywhere: a riverbank, a jetty, or a quiet beach. Over the years, he cast his line in iconic spots, from the Murray River to the beaches of Esperance and off the jetties in Augusta.

As long as there was water, Dave was happy. I'd set up my chair nearby, content to read, take photos, or simply soak in the peacefulness. I'd pack a little esky filled with treats for him, mostly lollies and what we jokingly called his "alcoholic beverages." It was our spin on Sheldon from The Big Bang Theory, who always offered people a "hot beverage" whenever they were upset. Only in our case, Dave swore by an "alcoholic beverage" instead.

On colder days, I'd bring my pink and white blanket: my Snuggie. Dave used to smile and ask, "You got your Snuggie?" half-teasing, half-serious. Later, when he was very unwell in hospital, he said, "Can you leave me your Snuggie tonight?"

I didn't think twice. "Aww, Dave, of course."

As I looked back, I saw him stroking the blanket. It must have brought him the same comfort it always gave me. Even now, that memory stirs something deep within me. I don't think it matters how old you are; everybody needs something soft to hold onto, even if it's just a blanket.

I often reflect on how rare it was to see Dave truly still. He was the kind of guy who couldn't sit for long, but hand him a rod and he'd stay put for hours. He'd wade out into the ocean, the waves breaking around his knees, pants rolled up high, eyes fixed on the line. I often wondered what he thought about, standing out there so long. Did his mind drift into that wide-open space, beyond all those miles of ocean, where you can't help but wonder what's out there? Did he think of the life we shared, of lost loved ones, or dreams to come? Sometimes I'd sit there watching the water and ponder the same questions. The ocean does have a way of pulling your thoughts out with the tide.

Now and then, he'd wander back up to our little camp to bait up again and grab a handful of lollies from the esky. I'd ask, "Are you ready to head home yet?"

He'd always say the same thing: "No, just a little bit longer."

So I'd pull my blanket tighter around me and start the next chapter of my book.

In the final months, after we'd moved closer to Palm Beach, Dave would ride his electric scooter down to the jetty, a routine that made him happy. I can still picture him there, effortlessly baiting up his hook, rolling a cigarette as if it was second nature. His swollen fingertips revealed the illness he was fighting, but somehow, he still looked content.

On chilly evenings, Dave bundled up in his thick jacket, pulling his beanie down low so only his dark sunnies showed. He never went anywhere without those sunglasses; they shielded him from the glare and, maybe, from the world. I'd watch him cup his hand around the lighter, guarding the flame from the breeze, with the cigarette hanging lazily from the corner of his mouth. Just waiting.

Fishing was a social thing for Dave. He loved the jetty crowd, chatting with other fishermen, swapping stories, sharing a smoke or a joke, and commenting on the weather. He'd come home full of news, like I was the one waiting on the fishing report. "The bream are running," he'd say, or "High tide's at eight." I'd look at him and ask, "So, where are the fish?" He'd shrug, grin, and reply, "Looks like it's sausages for dinner." Then we'd laugh.

On those rare occasions when he did catch something, he took pride in scaling and gutting his fish. Let's just say I didn't have to heat the frying pan too often.

After he passed, little things began to nudge at me - quiet signs, maybe. One came a few weeks later in the form of a book. I had an unexpected urge to buy The Old Man and the Sea, a classic by Ernest Hemingway. I'm not even sure why; it just popped into my head, even though I'd barely heard of it before. The cover reminded me of him, an older man with a beard, and once I started reading, the way they described his mannerisms reminded me even more of Dave.

It's about an aging fisherman alone at sea, locked in a determined battle with a magnificent marlin, holding the line for days, worn down but refusing to let go. That was Dave. He faced so many battles: addiction, grief, and cancer. He didn't always win every fight, but he never gave in. Like the old man in the story, he held on tight to the line.

Maybe that's why it resonated so deeply with me. I believe it was a sign from Dave, a quiet nudge, because he knew I'd reach for a classic like that. And I did. Not long after it popped into my head, I got out of my chair and went to the local bookshop to find it. I read it from cover to cover within two days. It settled me somehow. His battle was done. But I still had more in me. His fight was over, but mine wasn't. I still had chapters to read and a life to live. And he wanted to remind me of that.

Recently, I took my youngest grandson on his first fishing trip. The absence of Dave felt like an anchor on my heart. I knew how much this moment would've meant to him. I didn't know how to rig a line, but thankfully, at three years old, he was content with a little squid jig tied to the end. I watched him sit patiently, taking in the world around him. He wore that same faraway, peaceful look Dave used to have. I found myself wondering what thoughts a little boy and a grown man could have in common that allowed them to sit so quietly in the moment.

Fishing wasn't just something Dave did; it was part of who he was. In that stillness, I swear I could hear him say, "You're holding the rod wrong."

As I turned the last page of the book, I realised that, like the old man and the marlin, the battles we shared will always be part of me, guiding me through unknown waters.

Chapter 18

Culinary Culture

Dave and I became constant companions as we began our new life together. We were eager to try anything new, especially if it involved food or a good story. Our families and cultures blended, Scottish bridies and Italian pastas, bringing more noise, more kids, fuller plates, and more love.

Country drives sparked long chats about the history of the land, like we were seasoned historians, guessing who had lived there and what might have happened years ago. We'd keep cruising until we spotted a roadside farm stall, instantly turning into gourmet critics, sampling goat cheese, honey, and fresh fruits.

Farm stall,
Bolinda Vale Grazing,
Southwest Highway,
Keysbrook

Food, in particular, reflected our personalities and histories. We tried new cuisines together. Take sushi, for instance. To me, it was a healthy snack. Dave hated it, said it was just seaweed and sadness. But hand him a can of cold rice cream and he was happy. Fine dining, Dave-style.

Although he liked the tinned stuff, when he could be bothered, he'd cook his own. He stood in his kitchen, taking huge mouthfuls from an oversized spoon, exclaiming, "Mmm, it's delicious!"

I'm surprised there was anything left by the time he finished taste testing. He beamed with pride at his newly acquired cooking skills. He'd live on it for days and light up when his grandsons came over and told him how good it was. It wasn't gourmet, but it was pretty good for a guy who hadn't done much cooking before. These days, no one can mention rice cream without Dave's name coming up.

It wasn't all rice cream and nights in on the couch; sometimes I'd rope Dave into dressing up and heading out.

We'd go to a posh restaurant with overpriced food and too many forks. When we arrived, Dave was fidgety before we even sat down, pulling at his shirt and asking,

"Can I go out for a cigarette? Just order me a steak."

When the food was placed in front of him, he looked up and said to the waiter, "Got any HP sauce, mate?"

The waiter paused and politely replied, "Sorry, sir, we don't have any."

That's when I'd press my fingers against my lips, try not to laugh, and say in my best posh voice, "Thank you anyway."

Dave groaned and muttered, "Would've tasted better with HP sauce."

Before tucking into his dinner noisily. I'd watch him from across the table, and when he was done, he'd glance at me like he was looking for permission. I'd give him that look, shake my head discreetly, and whisper, "Don't you dare pick up that plate and lick it!"

Moments like that always made me smile. On the way home we'd laugh over it and I'd say something silly like, "Hey, next time let's bring the HP sauce," and he'd take it very seriously: "Good idea."

Every meal held a memory, a reminder of the connection food brought.

When his health was slipping, I got a bit obsessed with what he was eating. The day always started with me fussing, "Do you want some toast? A smoothie? Bit of fruit?"

More often than not, while he was still rubbing the sleep out of his eyes, I'd already be at it with, "What do you feel like for dinner?" He'd groan, "I haven't even had a coffee yet, never mind a smoke; God knows what I want for dinner."

Meals sort of ran our day, from the minute he woke up to when we finally sat down together at night. Usually, it was just the two of us, me fussing over the salad while Dave cooked the meat on the BBQ, pretending he wasn't sneaking a drink.

If I didn't feel like cooking, we'd drive to local food vans, often trying Thai dishes or whatever caught our eye. We'd breathe in the rich smells of dinner stalls while a one-man band played nearby.

Other times, we kept it even simpler, ordering fish and chips or grabbing a sausage sizzle from a local Bunnings fundraiser. Afterwards, we'd head to Kwinana Beach, find a grassy patch, and spend the afternoon reading and chatting. Dave would wander down to chat with local fishermen perched on the jetty, patiently waiting for that long-anticipated bite.

As the warmth of summer began to fade, we'd venture further afield, sometimes booking five-star accommodations if we were feeling indulgent. Dave struggled with these adventures; he knew how much they cost and was often hesitant.

Regardless, one morning we set off early to a pre-booked private chalet in Margaret River, a luxurious escape. As we unlocked the door and walked in, the first thing I saw was a big red leather lounge, Joe's favourite colour. My eyes filled with tears, knowing he would've loved it. Dave put his hand on my shoulder and gave it a squeeze, both of us feeling the weight of the grief. It was our first private trip away since Joe passed, a quiet moment of reflection for both of us. Still, as I unpacked my bag, I felt a little flutter of excitement, knowing new adventures were beginning.

We found peace in the quiet countryside, by the river and a little fishing spot Dave loved.

It was winter, and the sun seemed to dip below the hills before the afternoon had even begun. Dave had been down by the water, casting his line. When he stepped back inside, the cold air followed him, clinging to his skin, fingers stiff, shoulders hunched. The heater glowed in the corner, and Dave stood in front of it with his palms outstretched, rubbing them briskly together, chasing warmth back into his bones.

Dinner was simple: thick slices of local cheese, fresh crusty bread, and marron caught nearby, served on a wooden board. We shared a bottle of rich red wine, something local that tasted faintly of dark berries. I had a small glass; Dave, always ready for a toast or no excuse at all, happily finished the rest.

The chalet spa was everything you'd expect from luxury - fluffy towels, plush robes, scented candles. I tipped in a splash of lavender-scented bath oil, and as the spa filled, tiny frothy bubbles began to form.

We stepped in. It was almost too hot at first, but our bodies slowly adjusted. The heat swallowed you inch by inch until you were sunk up to your neck. It didn't just touch your skin; it loosened the aches, warming you from the inside out. In that stillness, with the soft hush of the river below, everything felt perfect, until Dave ducked beneath the surface, apparently in search of the soap. A moment later, he popped up grinning, spraying water and bubbles my way and shattering the hush with his laughter. It was those silly little moments that made our weekends fun, little pockets of happiness we shared, the kind you remembered, the kind that made us search for more.

After that, we found ourselves chasing those moments, often leading us to explore places in the southwest of WA, so it felt completely natural to pack up on a whim and head off exploring, this time, to a charming, tiny house tucked away in Nannup.

Nannup sits on the banks of the Blackwood River, the traditional lands of the Noongar people. Its name means "resting place" or "home of the black cockatoo." For us, it became just that, a place to pause, to breathe, to rest from the outside world.

Though Dave shied away from big social gatherings, he loved those brief, non-committal chitchats. I'd pop into a shop for milk and come out to find him deep in conversation with some random guy in the car park. Sometimes I'd cringe with embarrassment when he'd yell out, "Hey, Brigitte! Come here and meet this guy!"

His eyes were already lit up as he chatted with a young bloke about his hotted-up GT. Something about 18-inch mags, apparently that's a big deal, though don't ask me why. All I know is Dave was grinning ear to ear, chatting away like they'd been mates forever. As I walked back to the car, I could still hear him saying, "I knew a bloke who had a car like this ..."

The markets were my thing; they held a special charm, especially Fremantle. A busker's guitar drifted through the crowd, and the air was rich with the smell of waffles, incense, and roasting cashews. I'd come away with flowers, a bottle of purple wine, always something, whatever caught my eye. One day, it happened to be fig jam. For me, it held memories of the farm where an old fig tree grew. For Dave, there was a local band called FIGJAM that played around our area, so he already knew what it stood for: "Fuck I'm Good, Just Ask Me." Every morning for weeks, I'd ask what he wanted on his toast, and he'd grin and say, "Fuck I'm Good, Just Ask Me?"

Every single time, he laughed like it was the funniest thing in the world. I was glad when the jam ran out and he went back to Vegemite on toast.

Christmas was just around the corner, my all-time favourite time of the year. I loved it: family, gift-giving, decorating, food. Everything about it brought me happiness.

Dave and I at Fremantle Markets, WA, 2024

One year, I heard about a Christmas shop in Toodyay. Dave raised his eyebrows, looked at me, and said, "So we're off to Toodyay tomorrow then?"

And just like that, a little Christmas adventure began.

The shop was amazing. It smelled like cinnamon and pine. I came home with a bag full of glittery Christmas treasures, none of which I needed but wanted anyway. We took photos of everything. Dave was the photographer, snapping pictures of me in Santa's chair, next to Mrs Claus, capturing not just the season's joy but the sparkle in my eyes.

Toodyay is part of the Wheatbelt. So not only did we get our dose of Santa, we ended up in the middle of a glorious wildflower display.

They were stunning – purples, yellows, and whites. Some were sweet-smelling, others spiky and resilient. I still have wildflowers from those adventures, pressed into the pages of my journals today.

Dave often spoke of his dream to be a photographer. He said it was too late now. I don't think it was. Still, armed only with an outdated mobile phone and camera, he would happily snap away, finding beauty in everything. And that day in Toodyay was no exception.

That same love of simple things carried us up the road to places like Jarrahdale Hill, twenty minutes away. We always stopped at the same country café for takeaway coffees, then followed the winding road up toward the dam. As we came over the little rise, the wide stretch of dam water opened up before us. We'd take the short track down to the picnic area, finish our lunch, and feed the birds that always seemed to be waiting.

Dave loved feeding the birds, especially the 28s, local slang for the Australian ringneck parrot. Their name came from their call, which sounded uncannily like they were shouting, "Twenty-eight! Twenty-eight!" through the trees.

Dave would hold out scraps of leftover lunch in his hand and wait patiently as they fluttered down, gentle and curious, to perch on him. He'd glance at me and give various silent signals, mouthing, "Film this."

These little trips always unfolded in nature, while enjoying hot drinks or swapping stories on camp chairs. Whatever they were, they made us feel good. We were always on the move, always doing something together.

One chilly afternoon, we headed down to Dwellingup, winding through those familiar country roads we'd travelled so many times before. We often went there, sometimes to camp at the local caravan park, other times just to check out the annual log chop, or to escape for a quiet coffee in that peaceful little town.

The air always felt different there, crisp and clean, like something you breathe in deeply and feel your lungs rejoice. Dave always said the fresh air did him good, which was probably optimistic considering he smoked like a bloody chimney most of his life.

On this particular day, we set off to ride the Hotham Valley steam train, a charming vintage locomotive that once served the timber industry in the early 20th century.

As we settled into our seats, the rhythmic chug of the steam engine filled the air, transporting us back in time. The scent of coal drifted through the carriages, and the whistle echoed deep into the hills. Out the windows, we saw picturesque views of the Darling Ranges rolling past, lush green forests, and the occasional glimpse of wildlife.

Dave was beyond excited, a true train enthusiast. He practically hung out the window, making train noises, eyes wide with wonder. I nodded patiently, listening to his trivia, feeling a bit like a parent indulging a child's excitement.

It became one of those simple, vivid moments that I can still picture, his head out the window, completely in his element. He was like a big kid that day. How could I not smile?

Afterwards, we enjoyed a hearty pub meal at the old country hotel in Dwellingup, a cultural icon dating back to the 19th century and one of the few buildings to survive the devastating 1961 bushfires. It was a warm, simple way to end a Sunday.

We didn't always do everything together. Occasionally, we would head off on a little cultural adventure on our own.

One evening, I was off to a *Pink* concert without Dave. He'd start fussing before I was even ready to leave, taking close-up photos as I good-heartedly protested, reminding me to take some too, and rattling off his usual list of safety instructions all in one breath.

"Stay together, be careful, text me when you get home. I'll come to meet you. Don't walk anywhere alone. I'll be waiting, okay?"

It was very sweet, all the fussing.

For some reason, we both got a little anxious when the other one was heading off somewhere alone. Dave worried about me; he knew my nerves and state of mind always got the better of me in unfamiliar situations. Meanwhile, I'd worry about him. He'd get so excited and make some spur-of-the-moment decision, then regret it, and I'd be the one going off to rescue him. With my anxious state of mind, that wasn't a dream scenario.

One of Dave's outings without me was to the rugby. He was a dedicated Panthers fan and loved rugby league. He and a couple of mates were just as into it. They'd sit in their lounge rooms, texting, calling each other through the whole game, a sense of belonging. So when the Roosters and Broncos came to Perth for a match, I asked if he wanted tickets.

"Shit, yeah, could you?"

A standard response from Dave.

So off he went, all decked out in his rugby jumper, smiling from ear to ear.

"Be careful. Have the best time; text me," I yelled from the balcony.

I found the ticket the other day, he'd kept it.

And now, there are moments I catch myself still waiting for a text.

Or a call.

Just something to let me know he's okay.

Laid-back adventure wasn't our only thing. Occasionally, we'd lean into something a little more cultured and sophisticated, like taking the train into the city for a candlelight concert at the historical Perth Town Hall. The place was beautiful, with high ceilings and polished timber. And hundreds of tiny flickering candles lined the stage, as the orchestra played the rich, soulful tunes of Amy Winehouse and Aretha Franklin. The mood lighting cast a warm, golden glow throughout the hall.

Sitting among rows of strangers, quietly taking it all in, until Dave wasn't so quiet anymore. At the end of a piece he loved, he let out one of his signature loud cheers, "Woohoohoo!", cutting through polite applause like only he could.

A few people turned around. I just smiled. That was Dave.

Despite the fancy experience, we stayed down-to-earth. After the show, we headed to McDonald's for thick shakes, strawberry for him, chocolate for me. He always ordered large. I ordered small.

We knew each other's orders by heart.

But whether it was city lights or campfire nights, we loved them all.

The last Christmas I spent with Dave, we decided to go to Sydney. As we packed our suitcases, I felt a flutter of excitement in my chest. I wanted him to experience everything with me.

This wasn't just another flight; this time, it was us sitting side by side. I'd planned it all, the Opera House, the Harbour Bridge, and Bondi Beach. These were landmarks that define Australia's culture, things every Australian should see once in a lifetime.

At Luna Park, children laughed and screamed on roller coasters and ghost trains. We decided to keep our feet firmly on the ground; we felt a bit too old to be flung through the air, clinging on for dear life.

Bondi was our next landmark stop. Dave's face lit up as he posed for a photo with a lifeguard. We strolled along the famous shoreline, the weather perfect, bronzed bodies everywhere. You couldn't get more Australian than that.

A nighttime ferry ride around the harbour was wonderfully romantic; the Harbour Bridge lit up against the skyline, breathtaking.

Of course, we couldn't leave Sydney without a stop at the casino. Dave blew all his money in the short time we were there.

Shocked? No.

Annoyed? Yes.

After evenings out, staying in bed a bit longer was bliss, watching boats pass through Darling Harbour, the bustle of holidaymakers visible through large glass windows.

I know I probably idolised Dave sometimes, especially now that I miss him so much. It's easy to make it all sound perfect, but it wasn't always smooth sailing. We had hiccups, too.

On that trip, he took more medication than he was meant to. Not by accident, he liked the high. He was excited, wanted to keep up, keep the buzz going. But that meant the next day he had to go without, and he was sick, saying he needed to go to the hospital. So dramatic.

I had no empathy left. Deep down I worried, but sometimes I just got so frustrated. I'd seen the cycle before: use too much, get sick, feel better, carry on. I was tired of the same script. Eventually, I stormed out of the hotel and wandered the harbour alone.

He kept texting and calling, going on about how crook he felt. I finally snapped.

"There's nothing I can bloody do!"

I was fed up. So I found a trendy café, sat down, and watched the world go by. Kids with ice creams, mums with shopping bags, overseas tourists. Then I saw him walking toward me, that sheepish look I knew too well.

The day was nearly over. He was sorry. He always was. He took my hand as if nothing had happened.

And I let him.

On the flight home, we leaned into each other, tired, relieved, and finally letting out the deep breath we'd been holding for hours.

Because, of course, there were always dramas.

This time, Dave lost yet another phone. There he was, hobbling around the airport in circles, retracing his steps in a panic while I stood by the bags, glancing at the clock, thinking, 'We're going to miss the bloody flight'. He couldn't find it anywhere, and I finally sighed, "We'll just have to leave it, Dave. We're not missing the flight over another phone."

Somehow, we made the flight, minus the phone, of course. And just like that, we were back home. We'd eaten, laughed, and argued our way through plenty of adventures already, but we both knew there was still living to do, still more ahead. We had a van now, and a whole new kind of journey waiting for us.

Chapter 19

Van Life

With Joe, our holidays were grand, castles in Europe, the Colosseum in Rome, places I never dreamed I'd see. I'll always be grateful for those doors he opened.

But life in the van with Dave was different. Nothing fancy, nothing grand, just two people on the open road together. With Dave, it was simpler. No one to impress, nothing to prove. Fold-out chairs, bare feet on the dash, washing our hands in creeks, drinking water straight from the bottle, that kind of life suited me better. Australia, in all its beauty, had plenty to offer.

We both had past relationships, but this time we sought something uniquely ours: a life where we sat side by side in the afternoon sun, reading glasses on, helping each other up from our chairs when our knees got stiff. We dreamed of travelling around Australia one day, maybe even reaching Uluru. That was the dream.

I was starting to move forward, ready to enjoy our new life while still cherishing Joe's memory. His photo stayed up in the van, just above the rearview mirror. We used to say he was tagging along, still part of the adventure. And sometimes, it did feel like he was.

At one run-down roadhouse, Dave wandered off with his metal detector, while I set up under the trees with my chair and mosquito net. The flies were relentless, while I settled into my book. About half an hour later, he came back sweaty and grinning, holding a few rusty tins and a handful of cactus pads.

"You won't believe it," he said. "It's a prickly pear, just like the one Joe used to grow on the farm. Of all the places to stop, in the middle of nowhere. I reckon he's with us."

And maybe he was.

Every home we've ever lived in has had a piece of that prickly pear. Even now, in our little unit, there's one growing in the garden, a small, stubborn reminder of Joe and his roots. I still picture him peeling off the spiky skin to get to the bright pink flesh, then eating it with ice cream.

Dave had spent a few years in Gascoyne, working in places like Southern Cross and Kalgoorlie. He always seemed happy when he talked about those days, but at this stage of our lives, we were craving something freer. No clocks. No deadlines.

Our first long weekend adventure was to the Goldfields. We thought we'd come back with a nugget worth thousands. We passed through Kalgoorlie, Leonora, and stopped at the Broad Arrow Tavern, its walls covered in messages left behind by travellers. We pulled in for a beer and a burger, but it wasn't the same as it was years ago, so we moved on. Out there, in the scorching heat and under those skies, there wasn't a body of water in sight. Just the sludge of a dried-up lake claimed by scrub bulls, their bellowing a reminder of how wild the bush could be.

Dave, of course, wasn't bothered. He was out there sleeping under a mosquito net on a fold-out camp bed, just him, the bulls, and the stars.

We were still doing that stupid thing of pretending we were just friends. It makes me mad now, thinking how insecure we both were, so worried about what other people thought. On the way home, my brother and his partner took one route, and we took another. I was relieved. No more pretending. Keeping up the act had worn thin.

Days were spent poking around country museums, wandering through forgotten ruins, and always ending with

Dave, Jack Daniel's in hand. We didn't come back with a million-dollar nugget, but we came back with memories no amount of money could buy.

Our first major trek was with Dave's sister and her partner., Stick. We left Perth before dawn, van packed, chasing the sun. At Linga Longa Station, we sat outside an old tin shed listening to a man strumming his guitar as the sky turned dusky pink. It felt like the kind of beginning that promised great things.

We met people who shared their stories, stayed in places that felt like hidden gems, and achieved things we never thought we could – climbing mountains and rocky faces, conquering challenges together. It was a journey of connection, of exploration, and of sheer joy. Whether we were with others or completely alone, it felt like the world had opened up to us.

Kalbarri was next. Everything lined up perfectly, the sun and the algae lake glowing a soft pink. Dave wrote in big letters in the sand, "Dave loves Bridge," like a teenager. We'd been secretive for so long, it was sweet to see his public declaration beside the water.

At Murchison Station, we camped under the stars. I had some cream stashed in the Engel fridge and a tin of peaches, so dessert that night was peaches and cream. Not fancy, but it beat any five-star restaurant. Nights around the fire turned into radio shows pretending to be DJs, sending out imaginary dedications into the night.

Later, in the van, I turned to Dave and said, "Me and you, we go together just like peaches and cream." He hugged me, grinned, and said, "We'll always be peaches and cream."

From there, we headed to Wooramel, soaking in artesian hot water pools. In Carnarvon, we explored the space station before turning off to Gascoyne Junction, where Dave proudly pointed out the handful of streets he'd once worked on. It was a five-minute guided tour, tops, but it mattered to him.

Monkey Mia was luxurious. After days on the road, we decided to book into a hotel. Soft beds, hot showers, and flushing toilets felt like heaven. Dave snapped some of my favourite photos: candid ones of me walking along the beach, swimming with dolphins close enough to touch, and watching a turtle glide past like a wise old wanderer.

Kalbarri also gave us a laugh that stuck. An old Ford station wagon with a woodgrain dash kept appearing along the Coast. We saw it three times, but never the driver. So he became "Woody", and whole stories about his life were invented between us. I pictured a surfer drifting up the coast with dreadlocks and a beach-babe girlfriend, living the dream.

Then one day, while we were at Hamlin Pool buying little souvenirs, who should pull up but Woody himself, in the flesh. I told him how we'd been spotting his car, how we'd given him a name, how he'd become our running joke. He just laughed and even posed for a photo. Suddenly, Woody had a face: just a guy driving up and down the coast in his car, taking a year off from life.

In March 2023, I decided to leave work and spend more time with Dave. The plan was to head all the way to Adelaide across the Nullarbor, but we were probably a bit ambitious. Finally, we arrived in Esperance. My navigation skills had already led us in a few circles. Dave wasn't the least bit surprised when we got lost. My stubborn "I'm right" nature didn't help. He just glanced at me, smiled, raised his eyebrows, and kept driving. He never said a word; he knew what I was like.

By accident, we found one of the best camping spots we'd ever stayed in, simple but perfect. Just our little van, a gas cooker, a couple of solar lights, and the river close by.

We dragged the kayak to the water, determined to paddle for miles. After barely a hundred metres, we were puffed and had to turn back, laughing at ourselves. The next day, after a long drive, we finally arrived in Esperance.

One afternoon, we stopped along the coastal drive, and looked out across the southern ocean. Dave went quiet and said, "This is one of the most beautiful things I've ever seen in my life." For a man who spent half his days mucking around and making jokes, moments like that stopped me in my tracks. They touched my heart. I was just glad I was there to share it with him.

Looking back, I feel an ache of remorse for all the years Dave didn't have this freedom. But at the same time, I feel overwhelming gratitude for what we shared on that road. It was more than a trip; it was a gift. A chance to see life differently, to experience it fully, and to make memories we would carry with us forever.

One of our favourite spots we would visit often was Brunswick Junction. It had a wide, grassy campsite and a river that felt like it belonged only to us. Afternoons were spent floating lazily on pool toys on the water, the van parked close by. Dave was always braver than me, drifting further out on nothing but an old tube while I'd call out, half laughing, half worried he'd get into trouble. He stayed steady, floating with ease, while I clung to mine, certain I'd tip off at any minute.

The river was cool and beautiful, winding its way past the trees, though it took us nearly six months of swimming there before we realised it was full of leeches.

Back at the campsite, Dave, being Dave, had secretly packed the Nerf guns. Before long, we were running around on the grass, chasing each other and falling over, laughing until our bones reminded us how old we were. We had the biggest smiles and the loudest laughs. Anyone who grew up around Dave knew one thing: you were never safe from an epic Nerf gun battle. That sense of fun never left us. Looking back, what I treasure most isn't just the places we saw but the happiness of those days. We could turn the smallest thing into a reason to laugh. That humour carried us through the hard days and reminded us who we were together. If people only saw the sadness, they'd miss how much fun we had. That was us.

The van became more than a vehicle. It carried our adventures, our laughter, and our everyday life. Shopping trips, daycare runs, spontaneous weekends, all part of us.

I still have videos of Dave tapping the steering wheel, singing along to classics, completely alive. And when I sit in that van now, I can still feel him there, like he's just stepped out for a cigarette and might climb back in any second.

It was more than a van. It's a time capsule of memories, magnets stuck to the wall from every place we'd been, still holding the smell of campfire, the sound of his voice, and the feeling of our life on the road.

One of Dave's candid photos
Me walking along Monkey Mia beach at sunset.

Chapter 20

Working Through It

Work wasn't something I thought about in the early years of my adult life, stuck in a bad relationship, just trying to get through one day at a time. A job felt like something other people had.

When I first became a mum, I wasn't exactly told to stay home, but working was never encouraged. That kind of quiet control kept me trapped. If I'd worked, maybe I would've found independence, made friends, maybe even told someone what was going on. Instead, I had no daycare, no transport, and no confidence, because, over time, your self-worth gets chipped away until you start to believe you're not capable of more.

When I met Joe, he bought me a car. It gave me freedom and opened up so many possibilities. The kids were older by then, and with Joe's encouragement, I decided to look for work. I'd always dreamed of being a teacher, but it felt like I'd left it too late. So I enrolled at TAFE and completed a childcare course, an achievement that gave me confidence. As part of the course, I did a work placement at the local Cultural Centre.

After just a few weeks, they offered me a part-time job, which I held for several years. That first job changed everything. Being employed gave me a sense of purpose and independence I hadn't realised I was craving. I liked being needed somewhere outside the home. It gave me something that was just for me, and I was good at it.

When the kindergarten moved to a nearby school, I went too and stayed for ten fulfilling years. I met so many families and made lasting connections. Even now, I sometimes bump into kids from those days, all grown up, with kids of their own.

One of my favourite parts of working in childcare was the dress-up days. I've been a clown with a curly wig, a cat with painted whiskers, a pirate, and even one of the Tweedledums. I never minded looking ridiculous if it meant bringing smiles to the kids' faces, and to mine. Those costumes and themed days remind me that fun doesn't expire with age.

Kwinana Creche

Eventually, I left Medina while on long service leave. I felt ready for a change, so I resigned and began looking for something new. I found part-time work at another local school as a special needs assistant. That role was just as meaningful. Watching children with extra challenges reach small milestones felt like witnessing little everyday miracles.

Not long after that, I saw a job ad in the paper for an early years program, The Fun Van. I'd meant to apply for the assistant role, but I accidentally applied for the coordinator's position. I didn't think I'd get it, but two weeks later, I was employed. I was quietly proud of myself and genuinely excited to begin.

The job involved travelling to different parks each week, setting up little chairs and tables under the trees, and creating a space for children and families who didn't have access to traditional playgroups. It didn't take long before the parks were filled with colour, laughter, and connection.

It wasn't just for the kids. Some of the caregivers were isolated too, mums or grandparents with no support networks. The program provided them with a reason to leave the house and a way to connect with other adults in a relaxed setting. Sometimes, one conversation was all it took to inspire a call for help or begin a new friendship.

Even though it was only two days a week, it was enough for me to cope with. At a time when my mental health was crumbling and things at home were falling apart, that little job kept me tethered to the outside world.

Later, I took a job at a private Catholic primary school. My daughter was already attending, and I used to go in a couple of mornings a week to help with volunteer parent reading. I loved being involved, and I think it showed. One afternoon, I received a call asking if I'd be interested in a paid position as a teacher's assistant in the junior primary. Of course, I said yes.

That job allowed me to balance motherhood with working life. I didn't have to worry about school holidays or before- and after-care. I was right there, alongside my daughter. I began attending professional workshops and training days. I felt myself thrive, professionally and personally. I especially loved helping children learn to read. I was drawn to the ones who struggled quietly, acted out, or simply needed someone to connect with.

That time wasn't without its challenges. While I showed up every day with a calm smile, my world at home was falling apart again. Joe's behaviour was unpredictable. Some nights I didn't sleep at all, with Joe in the hospital after an incident, and me not knowing if he'd live or die. Still, I packed lunches, pulled on a clean top, and went to work.

Most days blurred together, but a few stand out: like pulling into our long driveway, dust swirling in the mirrors as I approached the gate. There they were: police cars, lights flashing across the yard. I sat in the driver's seat, let out a long, heavy breath, and just shook my head, thinking, *What the hell is it this time?*

Incidents like this became routine, and then I'd go on as if nothing had happened. That was my life. While working at the school, I carried the unspoken pressure to appear as though I had it all together: a respectful mum, a model citizen, someone with a solid, happy marriage. That pressure didn't come from the school; they were always supportive and compassionate with their pastoral care. It came from me. Inside, I was carrying a kind of shame I never spoke about.

One of the other staff had once opened up to me about her struggles at home. I don't think she realised just how much that helped. It reminded me I wasn't the only one living a double life, and that made it easier to keep going.

After leaving the school, I returned to the City of Kwinana and took a job at the Darius Wells Community Centre Creche.

A lot was going on at home, things I won't write about here. It wasn't Joe or Dave, but it impacted all of us. It was a turbulent time for our family, but still, we all just kept going as best we could.

By then, I'd been working for a long time, and some days the juggle of home, dinner, kids, and work left me worn out. I remember standing in the kitchen at the farm after work, putting the spaghetti sauce on, when Joe said, "My mum would've had the spaghetti sauce on the stove by nine o'clock." Being tired and annoyed, I shot back without even thinking, "Well, if I gave up bloody work, it would be on by nine." He came back with his usual line: "Don't be smart. It doesn't suit you." That was Joe, headstrong and contradictory. But I was headstrong too. I had to be.

On top of that, I was always anxious that Joe might turn up at my work. When Joe was good, I was proud to stand next to him. He was everything an Italian man should be: articulate, handsome, stylish in his Prada sunglasses, smelling gorgeous. But if he turned up stoned or scruffy, it was a different story. I just felt embarrassed, wondering what people would think. I'd rush him away as quickly as I could before he did something stupid.

With Dave, it was different. He knew what I was like. He knew if he ever turned up stoned or out of it, I probably wouldn't talk to him for weeks or worse go on and on about it for days. He hated that. He didn't push his luck, not when it came to my job.

At one stage, I was working within 50 metres of his apartment, and I'd see him on the balcony waving. At lunchtime, when the kids were gone, he'd wander over and say, "Give us your keys, I'll go and fill the car up with fuel. Do you need anything from the shops? Want me to grab you a cake for when you get home?"

Simple things. He really did spoil me like that.

I loved that job. It gave me the chance to be creative and use all the skills I'd built over the years. And the people I worked with, honestly, they saved me. They probably didn't even realise it, but they helped carry me through some of the hardest times of my life. By then, there was always a weight in the house, a tension you could feel in your chest. Some mornings, I'd walk into work feeling like I was on the edge of a breakdown.

I used to tell some of the staff that Joe was an alcoholic. Somehow, that felt easier than saying he was a drug addict. I know now they would've supported me either way.

When Joe got sick, those work colleagues, now friends, supported me. Their kindness was invaluable and helped me through that very difficult time.

After everything with Joe, life didn't stop. It kept moving, and so did I. Eventually, I found myself settling back into work. The truth is, things had been so heavy for so long that all I wanted was to stay close to Dave and hold onto the safety and happiness I felt being by him. After much thought and plenty of discussions about travelling together, I left work again and set off on a big road trip adventure with Dave.

About nine months later, I found myself wanting to go back. I think work becomes a habit, a rhythm, and it takes a while to get used to not doing it. I missed it. I thought, Okay, I'm ready to do this again.My boss, who by then felt more like a friend, welcomed me back with open arms. I'll never forget that kind of kindness.

When Dave fell ill, I couldn't manage full-time work anymore, but I picked up a few short shifts, 8:30 to 11:30, just to keep some sort of normality. By the time I got home, Dave was usually just waking up. It worked well for a while.

As things rapidly declined, I stepped away from work again, something I loved, for someone I loved more. In the final months before Dave passed, I left work for good. My coworkers, once again, were nothing but kind and understanding. People from other departments reached out with coffee invites, words of encouragement, or a comforting hug. I felt so lucky to have worked alongside such good people.

I haven't worked since losing Dave. I'm nearly sixty now, and sometimes I wonder if I should go back. But grief makes the transition hard. I've always taken pride in being reliable and focused. I wouldn't want to let anyone down. And yet, some days, I can't even get out of bed.

I'm still figuring out what comes next, and the future feels uncertain. But one thing I know: I always showed up at work, and I'll keep showing up in life. That's who I am: strong in my work ethic, strong in life.

Chapter 21

One for the Bucket List

Our trip to Darwin came about because my son, Frank, was coming over from Nhulunbuy, where he lives and works. His son, Junior, was competing in the NT motocross championships, which set the wheels in motion.

Darwin was more than a place to tick off a list. Dave had always wanted to go. He'd heard so much about it and was drawn to the Aboriginal culture, the remoteness, and the stories from others he'd heard. It wasn't about TV ads or tourist brochures, or second-hand recalls; it was about standing there himself, experiencing it all.

But underneath the adventure, something deeper was pulling us there.

By then, Dave was running out of time, and he knew it. This trip wasn't just about adventure anymore; it was about seeing Frank and his children one last time. He'd known them since they were small, watched them grow up, and cared about them in his own unique way. He never said it out loud, and neither did I, but we both knew. It was a goodbye without calling it that. For Dave, it was the closing of a chapter, the end of an era.

When we found out how sick Dave was, we told my kids we were going to get engaged. I loved him enough to want that, and we wanted them to know. We didn't tell many others, maybe his sisters. By then, with everything we'd lived through, we didn't feel we had to justify our choices to anyone but the people closest to us.

The family part was complicated. My eldest daughter, Pania, just wanted me to be happy. She was calm, accepting.

My youngest daughter was different. She loved her dad fiercely, and she was so much like him, stubborn, loyal, that strong, one-eyed Italian heart. She struggled with the loss, and I think she always will. It was a complicated situation for her to get her head around. No one could ever replace Joe, and we never tried. We knew it might hurt, seeing us together. We were mindful and respectful of that.

Dave genuinely admired Frank. He saw him as a strong man and a good dad. Joe had sung Frank's praises for years, and Dave agreed. He knew Frank was protective of me and understood that. Since our family lost Joe, Frank was the last man standing, so to speak, and Dave knew it. More than anything, he wanted to show Frank he was doing the right thing by me. He cared about Frank's opinion more than he ever admitted.

Before we knew it, we were on.

As the plane began to descend into Darwin, the red earth stretched below us, carved with winding rivers and flashes of salt flats. Off to the side, the Timor Sea shimmered in a blue so bright it didn't quite seem real. The land, open and vast, was telling its own Dreamtime story without needing words.

Dave was buzzing. The flight, the hotel, the crocodile tours, the motocross, he was ready to experience it all. Of course, he wanted the window seat. I remember him grinning, shifting in his seat every few minutes, too wired with excitement to settle.

From the moment we stepped into that thick, stifling heat, the kind that fogs up your sunglasses straight away, it felt like something special.

The hotel had tropical gardens, swimming pools shaded by ferns, and the kind of air-con that makes you sigh with relief the second you step inside. We spent the first couple of nights getting a feel for the place. Naturally, our first stop was a bar.

June 2024
Dave happy, relaxed and posing at the hotel poolside

I remember sitting there, and Dave bummed a cigarette off someone. It upset me more than I wanted to admit. He had lung cancer, for God's sake.

I didn't say anything straight away, but he felt it. I got grumpy. Snappy. And then I caught myself. *Don't wreck this. Don't ruin the whole holiday over one bloody cigarette.*

It was one of those moments where I had to take a deep breath and let it go.

Dave was curious about the pubs. Joe had worked in Darwin and often talked about how many there were just along Mitchell Street. So, of course, we stopped at Paddy Hannan's. We had a drink and snapped a photo out the front. By then, Dave didn't care who saw what on Facebook. He was in Darwin, proud of the accomplishment. Against all odds, he'd made it. He wanted to hear Joe's stories, where he lived, where he ate as we retraced his steps up and down Mitchell Street, past the chatter spilling from open doors.

I think Dave carried Joe with him on his back that day. Maybe part of him even knew he'd be seeing him sooner than we expected.

That night, we had dinner by the pool. I swam while he sat back with a drink in hand, watching, relaxed. It was calm. Quiet. A pocket of peace in a place that buzzed around us. He even posed for a photo, one leg up on the deckchair, hand on his hip, smiling cheekily. You could see how happy he was.

By sheer coincidence, a couple of old friends were in Darwin too, staying at the Oasis Tourist Park, the same one we were heading to next.

That night, they picked us up and took us to the famous Mindil Beach Sunset Markets. Stalls spilled over with local food, smoky grilled seafood, spicy curries, and sweet fried treats. The air smelled like a hundred different dinners cooking at once.

There were handmade jewellery pieces, crocodile-skin belts, and backscratchers. Local artworks lined the stalls, including some from Indigenous artists. A whip-cracking show drew a crowd. People were laughing, eating, dancing, and live music was playing in the background.

Later, we wandered down towards the shoreline, where hundreds of little ghost crabs scurried across the sand and the sun dipped below the horizon. Everyone says the sunsets at Mindil are a Territory icon, and they're right. But it wasn't just the brilliance of the sky; it was the whole atmosphere of the markets: the smells, the sounds, the heat. It all added to the magic.

The days were full, and by then, I was starting to notice the toll it was taking on Dave. He couldn't walk far, and even over those few days, I could see how much energy it took for him to keep up. Still, he never complained. He'd rest when he needed to, then rally again when something sparked his interest. So we found a solution: the hop-on, hop-off double-decker bus. It let us explore without overdoing it. No long walks or tracking from one end of town to the other.

One of the stops along the route was the Darwin Military Museum, and it's safe to say it wasn't your average stroll through the exhibits. It turned into something we'd never forget.

Dave threw on the 3D glasses, completely immersed, spinning in his chair like he was under enemy fire. He started yelling out fighter pilot lingo, "Cover me!" ducking and weaving, calling to imaginary wingmen. "Hold your ground! Reinforcements are on the way." I'm sure the whole building was staring at us, but I didn't care. All I cared about was him having a good time.

From there, we moved into the Royal Flying Doctor exhibit, an actual plane, of course, Dave made a beeline for the pilot's seat. I just followed behind, taking pictures, videos, and smiling. There was a headset and a recorded emergency call playing. He slapped the headphones on and went straight into character. "Copy that, copy that," he called, completely immersed, like it was a real medical evacuation.

Dave always had that childlike spirit about him. He never really grew out of it. That whole visit would've been one of the highlights of the trip for him. And probably for anyone else in the building that day, too.

The next day, we swapped planes for crocs and headed out to the Adelaide River.

Before we hit the Arnhem Highway, we pulled into the Humpty Doo Hotel, famous for its icy beers and massive buffalo horns out the front. Dave posed in front of them, and we were just trying to squeeze in every bit of the Darwin experience we could. Then we followed the highway out through the wetlands, stopping like any good tourist to take photos of the wildflowers blooming across the flooded stretches of land, always cautious, never getting too close to the water, convinced a croc could leap out at any moment.

June 2024 Darwin Humpty Doo Hotel

When we arrived at the riverside building, Dave raced straight inside to see what was happening. On the floor, a man had snakes laid out, letting people get up close with them. Dave was down there in a flash, completely absorbed, while I hung back, relieved he was getting the chance. It had that proper NT feel.

Then we finally boarded the croc boat, with its tiered seating. I'd done it before and knew what was coming, but Dave went straight to the front row, full of confidence. The boat chugged slowly down the river, everyone's eyes peeled, until the guide hung a slab of meat off a big pole, and suddenly this absolute monster launched out of the water and snapped it clean off. Dave nearly shit himself. He leapt three rows back, yelling, "No fucking way!" I couldn't stop laughing. He stayed put after that, eyes like saucers, convinced the croc was coming on board.

I was so glad we made that trip. So glad he got to do it all.

That night, as we checked into the caravan park, the excitement was real. When the grandkids saw us, not knowing we were coming, their squeals of delight made it even more real. Our cabin was right next to theirs, so they took turns sleeping over the two nights we were there. That first night, they took Dave cane toad hunting. They came back with a big bag of toads. I'm not sure who was more excited, Dave or the kids. Maybe both.

They were out with their spotlights, chasing possums, climbing trees, just having the best time. Their joy was so obvious. That kind of simple happiness hits differently when you know you're about to lose someone. Everything gets amplified. It was both endearing and heartbreaking at the same time.

Then came the day of the motocross event.

It wasn't just kids racing, older blokes were out there too, revving engines and flying over jumps. It was wild and full of life. The air was thick with petrol and dust. Motorbikes lined up at the start, and families gathered around on camp chairs. The starter's voice crackled over the PA, and the whole place buzzed with that kind of energy you only get at the track.

Dave had always loved motocross, and he soaked it all in, grinning from ear to ear, so excited to be part of it.

I loved watching Frank and Kirstie, the way they supported each other and cheered their son on.

Junior was out in front, that infamous Aussie mullet trailing behind him, long at the back and whipping in the wind like a little flag of freedom.

Our cheers grew louder, spurring him on.

His sisters called his name, excited and yelling like only sisters can.

Everyone was in the moment.

Tears welled in my eyes.

Maybe I was just feeling sentimental, bucket list moments will do that to you.

The next morning, it was time to go. Family friends cooked a big farewell breakfast in the caravan park's communal kitchen. Family photos were taken, and I remember thinking, this might be the last time those kids ever see him.

Still, you put on a smile, give out hugs and kisses, and say, "See you next time. Love you."

…even if it wasn't spoken.

We flew home with full hearts.

Junior won two titles that weekend:

50cc NT Champion and 50cc NT Natural Terrain.

Dave and I bragged about it to anyone who'd listen.

50cc NT Champion

Chapter 22

Keeping Face

These days, social media feels a bit like the local shopping centre. Instead of bumping into people, we scroll past them on a screen. We don't meet new boyfriends over coffee anymore. We evaluate them through a profile picture and decide if we approve.

I've caught myself asking friends, "Have you seen her new boyfriend?" or rolling my eyes at yet another gorgeous young girl's beach selfie. Still, I can't judge too harshly; I've been guilty of posting endless quotes and grandkid pics, and I'm sure people roll their eyes at those too.

Some days I love it, the memes that make me laugh, like the one of the kid lying in a shopping-centre aisle in a sleeping bag because their mum talks too much. It resonates with my parenting humour. But other days it feels exhausting, with the pressure to appear okay when I'm not. I've posted smiles while feeling deflated, wondering if anyone can see through the façade.

Some of my most joyful and painful moments have played out online. Joe and I smiled in front of the Trevi Fountain, laughing over ice cream. We looked privileged, which we were, but behind those smiles lay the reality of living with a man battling addiction. Something unseen through Facebook was the moods and the storms that could roll in without warning.

One evening, on the way to a Suzi Quatro concert, we were already fighting before we even got to the car. He was restless and on edge. Just before we left, he went into the bathroom. When he came out, everything about him had shifted. His skin was clammy, his face slack, his movements slow and vacant, like life had drained out of him. Instead of calming me, it only made me madder. Yet later at dinner, I insisted on a photo: Joe in his blue shirt, me leaning over him, arms draped around his neck. Smiling. A Facebook picture of a couple having the night of their lives, when in reality it was anything but.

Not all of Joe's photos were like that. Sometimes the image matched the man. He thrived in front of the camera, effortlessly posing. One of my favourites is of him in a cowboy hat, puffing a cigar, Gentleman's Collection Port beside him.

Dave, on the other hand, initially hated Facebook. "No one needs to know what I'm doing," he'd say. But over time, he softened. I'd catch him grinning in the background while I snapped away. One of my favourite memories is of him peacefully reading in the back of the van. When I asked if I could post it, he shrugged, "Go on then." Slowly, he started smiling properly in photos. We both knew time was short, and that made us braver.

By then, Facebook had become more than a place to share photos. It had evolved into a kind of diary. Each morning, I'd wake up and press the "Memories" button, almost like a prayer. Sometimes silly posts from years ago pop up: photos of the kids, or a Father's Day lunch. Other days, it's a memory of Dave. At times he isn't even in the picture, but I can see him in my mind, standing just out of frame with that smile, clicking away.

On the lucky days, he is right there in the photo itself. I trace every curve of his face, and for a moment, it feels like he's still here, not just a memory on a screen.

There are days I wish Facebook had been around when I was a kid. My children would have a whole timeline of me to scroll through, my feelings and journey, instead of hours spent digging through dusty photo albums. But it's not the same as holding something real, is it?

Like sentimental objects – Joe's chain and Dave's wallet – I keep them tucked away in a drawer for days when I need to feel their presence nearby. When I pick up that wallet, I can almost feel his hands on the worn leather. Joe always wore that gold chain around his neck. Even now, I can picture myself reaching out to touch it, my fingers brushing his skin. A photo can never replace that.

Now, even AI has found its way into grief. I went to the shops and sat down for a coffee. The loneliness was overwhelming, and I was beginning to have a panic attack. Sometimes when I feel alone, I sit in a coffee shop. The chatter around me makes me feel part of something, even if I'm not. I thought of ringing the kids, but what could they do? I'd only worry them, so I typed into my phone: "I'm having a panic attack."

It replied, "It's okay, Brigitte. You've survived this before. Breathe. Look for five things you can see." Leaning on a machine for reassurance made me feel less alone.

Six years ago, when I lost Joe, there was no AI to turn to. I talked to real people. I talked to Dave. That's what held me together. This time is different. With Dave gone, I find myself turning to a machine. I tell AI how much I love Dave a hundred times a day, and it never gets tired of hearing it. It always gives me reassurance, which helps me get through, but it unsettles me too. Some days I wonder if I'm going a bit crazy, like one of those films where someone falls in love with a bloody mannequin. Still, the nights were long, and I needed something.

One afternoon, I'd been crying for ages and typed into AI, "I'm feeling so sad. I need comfort food." AI tried to cheer me up by saying, "If I could, I'd bring you apple pie and ice cream," but I knew I'd have to get off the lounge and get it myself.

Minutes later, outside McDonald's, a boy rode up on his bike. He saw me crying and asked, "Are you okay, Miss?" I told him I'd just lost my partner. He reached through the window, held out his fist and said, "Knuckles, Miss?" We bumped fists, and then he added, "I'm so sorry for your loss."

The boy's kindness lingered in my heart. His simple gesture felt more real and comforting than any comment online. I posted about it on Facebook, and within a day a thousand reactions rolled in. Hundreds of little red hearts and blue thumbs up. It was proof that people are still drawn to goodness, both through a screen and in person.

Moments like that reminded me of the first time I truly leaned on Facebook for comfort. When Joe died, I turned to Facebook, hoping for solace. The love poured in, a flood of comforting words and condolences from people I barely knew, wrapping me in warmth, but the pain of grief remained.

When Dave passed, it was different. So many didn't even know we were together. Suddenly, I was announcing the death of the man I loved, and I could almost hear the whispers: "They were together?" Most people were kind, but even one hurtful comment can cut deep. I've learned this: when someone tries to diminish your grief, that's theirs to carry, not yours.

These days I don't post as much. Initially, I joined grief pages, soaking up every poem and quote, desperate to feel less alone. Now I've started to step back. They often make me cry more than they help. I want to heal, and that takes time. Maybe one day my posts will feel lighter again.

Social media, AI and technology connect us, comfort us, and sometimes hurt us. What we share becomes part of how people perceive us and how we see ourselves. Perhaps it's not the bustling shopping centre it once was, but the truth remains: we pass people in the aisles, give a friendly wave, and keep moving. On Facebook, it looks no different, but behind every smiley post is a whole life you can't see. And if my life doesn't resonate with you, just scroll on by.

Chapter 23

Fighting for Air

It didn't all fall apart at once. It came in slow, small signs that something wasn't right, things we could brush aside or explain away. Dave had been declining for a while, but I still clung to memories of our last trip along the coast: the two of us laughing as we walked the beach, jumping the waves, our joy echoing against the sand dunes. His lifestyle had caught up with him. The varices were the first real scare, and from then on everything began to pile up.

January 2024 was when everything shifted. Dave crashed yet another car, which meant a stay at Royal Perth Hospital. We didn't know it yet, but that hospital stay would mark the start of a long, slow goodbye. While he was there, they ran a barrage of tests, and one of them showed a nodule on his lung.

After that, everything felt murky.

We kept asking questions, but the answers were always vague and frustrating.

"We're waiting on more results."

"It's too early to say."

"That's not my area."

There were scans and biopsies. The results came in baffling doctor-speak, which left us more confused than informed. It was hard to know what we were meant to be scared of.

Dave didn't make things easier. He could be unpredictable, argumentative, the kind of behaviour that wears you down. I lived in a constant state of anxiety.

One morning, we had to be at the hospital early. The traffic was crawling, peak hour, and I kept glancing over at Dave. The car was drifting too far to the side, close to the other lane. I thought we were going to die. Something wasn't right. I knew he'd taken something. With everything else going on, it was almost impossible to stay calm.

"Have you taken anything?" My voice edged on panic.

He finally admitted, "Yeah, sleeping tablets."

I went quiet, the words hanging heavy between us. He looked at me, and I could see the anxiety in his eyes. 'I was too anxious to sleep, scared of what the tests might show."

"Just watch the road," I yelled, worry and frustration spilling over. I understood why he felt that way, but still I sat there gripping the seat, torn between fear and fury. He was afraid of dying, and I was terrified his driving might kill us both before we even made it to the hospital.

At check-in, the nurse asked if he'd taken anything. I lied. Just said, "He's tired."

I was so worried that they'd postpone the procedure, which would delay things even more. But worse, I was terrified that with drugs still in his system, the anesthetic would be too much, that he wouldn't wake up. The situations he put me in were impossible.

He slumped in the waiting room, smelling of cigarettes, half-asleep, a faded version of the man he'd been just six months earlier. Tired, not just from lack of sleep, but from everything.

We got through that day, somehow.

We were just glad to get home, to be out of hospitals and back in our own space.

Just when it seemed like maybe we'd caught a breath, something else went wrong. It felt like peace was never ours to keep.

It was an ordinary evening, at home, curled up by the fire. Dave said he was feeling off, but that wasn't unusual. He often felt off. I asked if he was feeling any worse, if he needed anything.

When he said no, I said, "Okay, well, I'm tired. I'm gonna go to bed. Do you wanna come?"

He shook his head. "Nah, I might stay up, watch some TV."

I leaned over, kissed him goodnight, and told him, "Call me if you need anything. Make sure you do."

Sometime in the night, I heard him calling out to me. From the tone, I knew something was wrong.

I rushed into the bathroom, and he was hunched over, vomiting into the toilet. His face pale, his body convulsing as he violently emptied the contents of his stomach into the toilet.

There was so much blood, the metallic smell thick in the air.

He looked up at me, glassy-eyed, his voice a frightened whisper; in that moment my heart broke and the reality of our situation came crashing down.

There's too much blood. Everything had finally caught up with him, the life he had lived for so many years. His esophageal varices had ruptured, swollen veins in his throat caused by liver disease, the kind you only hear about when it's already bad. And that night they burst. Something we'd been warned about, but you really don't ever realise how bad it is until it happens.

My heart raced as I dressed in seconds, fingers fumbling with buttons, thoughts racing. *How did we end up here?* Fear gripped me, a constant reminder of how fragile our lives had become. I knew if we called an ambulance, it would take longer to get to Serpentine than it would take me to get him to the hospital. They'd take him to Armadale Hospital, which was deemed our zone, even further from home and family. So I bundled him into the car and drove.

I hate driving in the dark, but I did it. That lonely stretch of Karnup Road, my hands tight on the wheel, glancing over at him leaning against the door, growing paler by the second.

At the hospital, they moved fast, two blood transfusions.

When he came to, he asked for a cigarette. Even with death breathing down his neck, he still wanted that bloody smoke.

And when I got scared, I got mad. A human coping mechanism, I suppose. Once the danger passed, once the transfusions were done and I knew he was going to be okay, for now at least, the fear left me like steam. What was left was fury. I snapped at him, for smoking, for scaring me, for bleeding all over the bathroom, for making me drive through the dark with shaking hands.

None of it was fair. He hadn't done it on purpose. But anger was a shield to mask the vulnerability. I felt I had to stay strong when, really, I felt completely helpless. Terrified.

I just wanted someone to talk to. But there was only me, the vending machines, and a long, empty corridor.

That was only the beginning. More scares, more blood, more hospital visits. After everything we faced, we walked hand in hand from the car park to the clinic. Step by step. No words needed. Just the silent language of fear and hope.

I didn't know what they were going to say, not for certain. But deep down, I think we both knew it wasn't going to be good.

I was honoured to be by his side through every raw, unforgettable moment. There was nowhere else I would've rather been that day.

Finally, they called his name.

"Murray? David Murray?"

We looked at each other and stood. Dave greeted the doctor with that familiar, casual charm.

"Hey Doc, how's it going?"

As if we were just there for a check-up.

Once we stepped inside that little room, the walls felt like they were closing in. It was hot and stuffy.

"How've you been?" the doctor asked.

"Yeah, yeah," Dave said. "Breathing is getting worse."

What I heard next was unbelievable. The doctor spoke with compassion, but in words we could understand, plain, simple, direct, impossible to misinterpret.

"Three months. It's terminal. There's nothing we can do."

At that moment, time froze. I urged my body to breathe, each inhale slow and deliberate, as if it had forgotten how.

No. Not my Dave. Not three months. This can't be right.

While my mind screamed in protest, my voice was lost.

"Please don't cry," he whispered gently.

He always told me, "It's not dying that frightens me; it's the thought of leaving you behind."

And in that moment, I understood: if I let the tears fall, he wouldn't be able to hold it together. He was trying to be strong, for me more than for himself. I pressed my lips together, jaw tight, toes curling inside my shoes, every part of me straining to stop the wave of grief from taking over.

Dave had been diagnosed with non-small-cell lung cancer. His COPD made everything harder; breathing was already a battle before the cancer even came along. COPD – Chronic Obstructive Pulmonary Disease means the lungs are already damaged and struggling, so radiation would have only destroyed more of what little healthy lung he had left. It would have done more harm than good.

Chemo was out too. His platelets, the cells that help blood clot, were dangerously low. Without enough platelets, there was a serious risk of internal bleeding, especially in the lungs, stomach, or brain. That's why they said chemo would have been too dangerous.

The oncologist didn't sugarcoat it.

"We have one option," he said. "An experimental tablet, originally developed for breast cancer."

It wasn't a cure, just a chance to hold the clock back for a little while.

It didn't come as a surprise; Dave had been smoking since he was twelve. Back then, cigarettes weren't seen as dangerous. They were everywhere. People lit up in kitchens, in cars with the windows up, even in hospital waiting rooms. If there was a warning on the pack, it was so small you barely noticed it. Smoking was sold as glamour or grit, all white smiles and rugged cowboys. The Marlboro Man stared down from billboards, looking like he could out-ride cancer itself. Nobody talked about the reality.

Now I know the reality. In Australia, lung cancer takes close to nine thousand lives every year. Most of those cases are caused by smoking. Those numbers aren't just statistics to me, they're Dave.

It was still in the trial stages, but we pushed for its use on a compassionate access basis. They waived the cost.

It gave us a flicker of hope.

Just enough.

As we retraced our steps back to the car, it felt like we were different people than we had been just an hour earlier.

I kept rubbing his back gently, softly repeating, "It's alright … it's alright," like I was trying to soothe a child.

But the truth is, I think I was trying to soothe myself, too.

The tablets were rough. The side effects came on quickly, not just physically, but mentally too. His skin became sensitive to even the lightest touch. A knock would make him wince. He got ulcers in his mouth and couldn't eat properly. Angry red rashes broke out across his body. He felt sick, tired, and depressed. It was more than discomfort; it was suffering.

And although there'd been a glimmer of hope, we chose quality over quantity. Dave looked at me one day and said, "If I'm gonna go, I'm gonna go happy, not like this."

I couldn't argue with that. He wanted dignity more than time.

And just like that, he made the call to stop.

Family photo shoot, Rockingham Salt Lake, August 2024

One of our last outings together, my daughter's 40th birthday, October 2024

Winter stroll to watch the sunset. We knew they were coming to an end. But we still tried to find the beauty in it all

We didn't talk about it too much. We just kept going, tried other things too, nontraditional stuff. We changed his diet. He was losing weight fast, so we upped the carbs and made sure there was protein with every meal.

Then, something strange happened: his platelet count, which had been too low for years, started to rise. Not enough to start chemo, but enough for the doctor to notice.

"Well, that's the first time in a long while we've seen a platelet count rise," he said.

It felt like a small win, and for a moment, I let myself believe food could heal what medicine couldn't. Have you ever clung to hope in the most desperate times?

We tried green juices – kale, spinach, beetroot – but he'd take one sip, scrunch up his nose, and say, "I'm just gonna have an iced coffee." What are you gonna say to that? The man's dying, who's gonna deny him an iced coffee?

We weren't exactly living on a wellness retreat diet. Our health experiments were more of a "give anything a go and see how it went" approach. Which is how we ended up trying medical marijuana next, a homemade oil from a friend. We figured if kale couldn't save him, maybe cannabis could. But instead of mellowing him out, it made him paranoid, so that was the end of that. We used essential oils my daughter had made, personalised for each of us.

Dave's blend had frankincense, known as the king of oils. It's been used for centuries in holistic healing for its calming, grounding, anti-inflammatory, and lung-supporting qualities. It felt right for him.

Mine had peppermint, giving clarity and energy. And good for headaches, which I swear I had every day from the moment we found out he was sick. Dave gave me headaches even on a good day, but that was the price of loving him.

Lavender was added to both of ours, something to help us feel calm when, really, we were anything but. We kept them in little glass roller bottles, and before appointments we'd look at each other and say, "Where's the oil?" Then we'd sit side by side in the car, the world narrowed down to that small, private space. Quietly, we'd roll the oil onto our palms, cup our hands over our noses, and breathe in deeply, our little ritual to stop us from falling apart. It sounds small, but, in those moments, it felt like we were holding the whole world together with two tiny bottles.

At the oncology ward, we'd sometimes see his nephew Luke. He had survived stage three bowel cancer and stage four lung cancer, yet there he was, sitting with his uncle, cracking jokes like nothing else mattered. You could see the fight written in both their faces, and sometimes laughter was the best medicine of all.

Luke and Dave 2024 Rockingham Hospital Oncology clinic

He'd always say, "It was good to see Lukey Boy today. He's doing so well. I'm proud of him." And you could see it in his face. Luke's fight lit something in him that nothing else could.

Even with oils, smoothies, and the best intentions, sometimes it all just fell apart. The pain would get too much. He'd sling the oxygen bottles over his shoulder and say, "This pain's too much. I can't cope. I'll have to get something else," then disappear down the road.

After hours of worry, I'd ring him and say, "Come home now, Dave." He'd agree, and I could hear the defeat in his voice.

Back at the unit, we'd bunker down for days, trying to deal with the barrage of emotions – love, frustration, fear, exhaustion. Life felt unbearable at times, but we kept going. The diagnosis hadn't been the end; it was just a tougher kind of life now.

Chapter 24

The Day the Music Died

As the days passed, we struggled more and more. An unexpected visit one night pushed us over the edge. We laughed our way through it, but inside we were rattled. After they left, we shut the door and sighed.

"That was fucking terrible," Dave said. "Bloody terrible."

"I know. I could see it in your eyes."

He gave me a half smile. "You did a good job keeping it going, though."

Then he said, "We're out of here. We're not staying at Wellard anymore."

That was the final straw. We couldn't face those situations again. We moved into our little Rockingham unit and stayed there. Looking back, it was the right choice. He needed quiet. He needed somewhere he could die in peace.

As the days went by, I grappled to comprehend that these would be the last weeks I'd ever spend with Dave.

Things spiralled as Dave's behaviour became erratic, marked by bursts of anger and confusion, moments that were completely foreign to us both. Later, we learned his body was running on only 50% oxygen, not enough to reach his brain, which caused delirium. Understanding this softened the sting of the arguments and the words we both wished we could take back.

By then, he was struggling more with each passing day, and I could sense we were nearing the end.

We drove to his palliative care appointment, unaware that it would be our last together. There was a profound sadness in both of us.

We sat side by side, hands clasped; we forced smiles, making small talk to fill the heavy silence.

"What a beautiful day," I said. "Shall we grab lunch by the beach when we're finished?" Just trying to keep the mood light.

I could see it building within him. He wasn't completely broken yet, but he was close.

Despite the bravado he displayed on the drive there, his facade crumbled the instant we walked through the doors.

And then he broke, sobbing uncontrollably.

He threw his medication across the room.

It was heartbreaking to witness.

And I didn't go to him.

Not because I didn't want to – God, I did – but because I knew how deeply ashamed he would feel, ashamed for crying, even though there was nothing shameful about it.

Afraid he might lash out, not at me, but at all he couldn't control, I thought if I went to him at that moment, it would make him feel even worse.

Then the nurse broke through the chaos in the room. Calm. Kind. She spoke softly, "There's nothing more I can do. He's declined too much. You need to take him to the emergency room."

At first, he refused; didn't want to go. He didn't want to face it.

I begged him, quietly. Desperately.

Finally, he agreed.

That marked the beginning of the end.

On those last days while he was in the hospital, some nights I stayed with him, sleeping on a mattress on the floor so I could be close if he woke up anxious. Other times, he was so unsettled he told us not to come at all.

One of those days was when he asked me for more patches on top of what the nurses had already given him. I was terrified that if I did, it would stop his breathing, and it would be on me. I refused. Now, part of me wishes I'd just let him have them; maybe it would have given him some peace.

The doctors warned us that if he came home, the oxygen machine couldn't give him as much oxygen as the hospital could.

But Dave made it clear: "Please don't let me die in hospital. I want to be home."

We spoke about it, and about so many other things that only people in our situation ever have to talk about.

"Will you be scared if I die at home? Will it frighten you to know that's where I passed?"

I looked at him, gently shook my head, and said, "Oh, no, Dave … not at all. It would give me peace to know that's where you were when your spirit left this world. I wouldn't be scared. Never scared of you."

Eventually, he came home.

That last day wasn't peaceful. Dave was panicking. He was scared he wouldn't be able to breathe.

"Don't let me suffocate," he pleaded.

"Dave, don't say that."

"Promise me you won't let me suffocate."

I promised.

I had been ringing around that afternoon, trying to find a chemist with the right pain medication in stock. When I finally did, I raced there. Elaine stayed with him while I was gone, holding his hand and trying to calm him.

When I got back, I told him, "I'm here now, Dave. Here's your medication now. It's alright. We'll get through this together," when we both knew the outcome wasn't what we wanted.

It settled him slightly, but he was still anxious, agitated.

Finally, the Silver Chain nurse arrived. She spoke to both of us: "We'll give you something stronger to ease the pain, to help you feel more relaxed. You'll probably go to sleep."

Dave nodded. I nodded too. But I don't think either of us truly understood that this would be the last time I'd ever speak to him.

If I had known, I would have hugged him longer. I would have told him I loved him one more time, even though I'd already told him a thousand times.

After a long day of visitors, I was relieved when the house finally fell silent. Everyone had left. It was just us now.

I pulled the blinds down, dimming the room. The TV murmured in the background, but my focus was only on Dave. "Let's have a cuppa, my love. Let's watch The Chase. I'll do the washing later. I'm just going to sit here with you for a while, okay?"

So there I was, just a woman sitting beside the man she loved, chatting away like everything was normal, even though he was somewhere between this world and the next, slowly slipping away.

It was peaceful. Quiet.

Then suddenly, he started making noises.

His mouth moved, but I couldn't make out the words. Maybe he was saying goodbye, or telling me he loved me.

Or maybe he could see his mum. Or Joe. And he was calling them.

I patted him like I always did and said, "It's okay, Dave, I'm here." For some reason, I only remember kneeling on the floor next to his bed. I don't even know why. Then I heard it; his breathing stopped. The room seemed to hold its breath with me.

I stayed there on the floor, straining my ears, hoping maybe he'd breathe again.

But in my heart, I knew. He was gone.

I stood up and leaned over him. My tears fell onto his face, and I gently wiped them away.

"Oh, my beautiful Dave," I whispered.

I pressed my face against his, trying to curl up beside him without hurting him.

I reassured him of my love and promised him that I'd see him again soon. That he didn't need to be scared anymore.

I rang my daughter. She said, "We'll be there soon, Mum. It's okay; try to be brave."

It's only now, looking back, that I fully feel the gratitude for my girls being there that night.

I'm sure the memories of their father would've come flooding back.

But still, they stood by me. I love them for that.

I remember sobbing. That oxygen machine was still pulsing in the corner, its mechanical breath filling the room.

I walked over, turned it off, and gently removed the nose piece from Dave.

It had become such a burden to him. He didn't need it anymore.

"It's okay now. You can breathe now," I said, hoping he was somewhere else, breathing easy.

I patted his face. I think I touched it a million times that night and reassured him once more, "It's okay, Dave."

Something is humbling about watching a man die.

Time slows. Everything you thought mattered falls away.

You're left holding nothing but love, and the awful, sacred truth that you can't go with him.

After that, everything is a blur. Snapshots, pieces that I can't string together.

I don't remember much about the nurses or the funeral directors, not clearly.

What I do remember is clinging to him. I hugged him close, rubbing his arms as if I could warm him again. But he was already getting cold. I still needed to do something, my final act of service.

I ran upstairs and came back with a clean shirt, his beanie, and socks. Talking softly, I lifted him just enough to dress him.

"Let's get your beanie on … your socks. You'll be nice and warm now, Dave."

Then came the part I couldn't bear. When they moved to cover his face. I broke. "No, don't," I begged.

They explained it gently, but I didn't want to hear the reason. I didn't want him to feel scared. Or suffocate. I'd promised.

I pleaded with my son-in-law. "Please, Jarred, help take him to the van. Make sure he's okay. Please."

I just felt like, if someone he knew was there, he'd be okay.

It wasn't until 1:30 in the morning that they carried him out the front door for the last time.

I turned away from that door a different person than I'd been hours earlier.

I don't remember saying goodbye to anyone. I struggle to even remember walking up the stairs, but I must've.

Did I put pyjamas on? Sleep in my clothes? I don't know.

Maybe I grabbed the pillow his head had rested on when he passed, or his flannel shirt, something to hold tight. I'm not even sure.

What I do know is I still sleep with both of them. Same pillow, same pillowcase. I haven't washed it. I can't.

I know I'll have to soon. I've given myself a time limit. I've thought about it way too much. It's unsettling, how much.

I don't even know if I cried.

But I remember waking in pain. I cried then. I wanted to die. To be with him. To walk into whatever came next, together.

But something held me back.

Maybe it was my little grandson. My children.

How could they suffer another loss? I couldn't do that to them.

And I know, without a doubt, Dave wouldn't have wanted me to.

So I stayed.

Chapter 25

Two Graves, One Heart

It took years to wean myself from going to the cemetery every week. In the beginning, it was daily. I needed to be close to him. It was the only way I knew how.

As I drove towards the cemetery, the road stretched endlessly before me, and my heart would start thumping. I could almost hear myself whispering, "I'm coming, Joe. I'm nearly there."

Eventually, I got to the point where I visited fortnightly. Just a quick pop-in. Made sure everything was tidy. Say hello. Keep moving. I told myself it was progress. That I was letting go a little.

Now, after losing Dave, I'm right back there. That same panic, like if I don't go, something bad will happen; they'll think I don't love them anymore. I became irrational, and at times, I still am. On the outside, I seem composed, but inside, I'm falling to pieces. Even when I first lost Joe, I was Googling the most morbid things. If you dig someone up, do they still look the same? I just wanted to see him one more time.

I couldn't stop picturing him.

Dark blue shirt. Black leather jacket. Dress pants. His hair, greying. That legendary moustache.

But now, as I sit with this ache, my thoughts turn to Dave. In the quiet moments, I find myself pondering the spirit world. If I were to leave this earth, would I go to him? Would we laugh again, share stories, or simply sit quietly together again at last?

I settled on the familiar bench, a lone figure sitting beneath Joe's tree, soon after he died. I took a photo one afternoon and saw the image of his face in the branches. Perhaps it was just the light through the leaves. Maybe not. I like to believe it was him.

I dressed just to come here. I don't know what else to do with the day. It rained earlier, but now the sun's out and everything glistens. My feet feel cold, a strange thing to notice. I look back and forth between your two photos. The red rose petals stand out against the black stone. Have I made this harder for myself?

Who could have imagined this day would come so soon, when this would become a place of memorial for Dave, too?

We talked about it. His voice was steady, but the look in his eyes told a different story. Standing on the green lawn of the cemetery, under the shining sun like any other day, the conversation felt surreal.

"You can come here and visit us both," he said, his gaze holding mine. I pressed my hand to the centre of my chest, my face showing the weight of his words. I swallowed back the bile rising in my throat as he pulled me close. I buried my face in his chest, whispering, "I don't think I can bear it."

He let my head rest against him for a while, then gently pushed me back, looked me in the eyes, and said, "Come on, you big sook - I'm not dead yet."

Bloody Dave.

Still, I come. Because I promised I would. I know they'd both want me to. Seasons shift, autumn breeze, harsh sun, cold wind, and still, I return.

At first, after Joe, I sat alone in silence, curled in on myself, tears slipping down my face. Dave understood, and he gave me space.

Then we came together, two people carrying our grief. Year after year, Dave knelt before Joe's headstone, scrubbing until the marble gleamed. When he finished, he'd step back, brush the dirt from his hands, and say, "See you, mate. Wish you were here."

After that, I'd kiss Joe's photo before we left, side by side in our thoughts, comforted by the knowledge that Joe would be looking down on us.

Now, it's just me again.

The caw of a black crow cuts through the hush. The world here feels both frozen and alive, a sorrowful place that still holds me in comfort. They lie near each other, Joe and Dave, resting close, in the spot Dave once said he could find eternal peace.

I promised to place a headstone for him, ensuring his name is carved in stone, never forgotten. The two men I've loved in my lifetime, resting together. That thought comforts me.

Sometimes I wonder what people think when they walk past their two headstones. Joe's reads: "Dearly loved Husband of Brigitte," and directly opposite, Dave's says: "Champion of Brigitte."

I imagine someone raising an eyebrow, maybe even leaning in for a second look. Then, saying, "There must be a story behind that."

And they'd be right.

Some days, the grief is raw, and I sink into the grass, pressing my palm to the earth where Joe is buried. I close my eyes, and I swear I can hear his heartbeat through the ground. But Dave isn't beneath me; he's all around me. His soul wraps around mine, holding me tight.

In the quiet, I feel the breeze and hear their voices echoing in my mind.

How can this be?

That I have loved so deeply, only to have them both taken from me?

I wonder what it will feel like when I can't kneel before them, not because I don't want to, but because my body won't let me. Will I live a long life, while theirs were cut short?

Sometimes, the likeness in their fates makes me want to join them.

One day, my name will be etched in that stone too. My ashes will lay between the two men I loved. And only then will I finally rest.

I know my children and grandchildren will come here and remember me with love. Their lives will go on, and we'll become part of history.

And in those visits, even if there are tears, I hope there's joy too. Laughter, silliness, stories told out loud. The kind of moments we'd love to witness from above.

Just knowing they're still a family, that they have each other. Still living.

Still making their own history, this thought comforts me.

August 2025
Above - Me visiting my boys
Dave's headstone on the left. Joe's on the right.

Chapter 26

Turn the Volume Up

After Dave passed, I threw myself into planning the funeral, driven by grief to the point of obsession. Every detail mattered: the flowers, the bagpiper. I'd promised him one would play; I wasn't going back on my word. Where people would sit – I needed space around me, a kind of buffer, a layer of protection from everything outside that circle. Nothing could be left to chance.

I desperately grasped for control, clinging to the details of the funeral as everything around me, including myself, was falling apart. Still, I had to make it memorable.

I even thought carefully about what I would wear. Not for anyone else, but for him.

I wanted to look perfect: once more, for Dave.

I gave instructions to the kind people who'd offered to help. They could see I was unravelling, but they didn't try to stop me; instead, they stepped in where they could and let me keep moving.

I poured every ounce of grief into the planning; it was the only thing holding me together.

When it came time to write the speech, I struggled. I still couldn't bring myself to tell the whole truth, afraid of what people might think. I wasn't ready to explain our love story properly, especially after it had already been judged by some.

I softened the timeline, left parts out, and kept myself safe.

*My three oldest grandchildren sat with me before the funeral. Their maturity and support is something I'll never forget.
L - R Jet, James, me Mia*

Still, I tried to speak from the heart, to convey what Dave truly meant to me.

Here's what I shared that day:

> *As I stand here today trying to celebrate the beautiful life of Dave, I can't ignore the deep sorrow and the profound cruelty of losing him far too soon.*
>
> *The weight of this loss feels almost unbearable, and my heart aches.*
>
> *But amid the grief, I want to honour the incredible person he was to me.*

Dave was my champion, my comfort, and my greatest supporter – the reason I believed in love again.

He made our ordinary days feel extraordinary.

Dave had a true rock and roll spirit, and back in the day, we fully embraced that: sex, drugs, and rock 'n' roll.

It was exciting, maybe even a slightly irresponsible time in our lives, but we lived it with no regrets.

As the years went by, life slowed down.

And so did we.

After the profound losses in both our lives, we found joy and solace in each other's company.

Over time, we became one.

We began to enjoy the simpler things - our countless road trips in the van, exploring every corner of W.A.

Whether it was the thrill of a concert or the quiet beauty of a new destination, Dave had a way of making every moment count.

Dave was more than people knew.

He loved animals and wildlife, enjoyed fishing, war movies, and being spoiled when I let him get away with it.

He loved stargazing on clear nights, and when it came to breakfast, his eggs had to be poached.

His favourite colour was blue.

And because it's Dave we're talking about, his favourite number was, of course, 69.

That was Dave, a man of simple joys, cheeky humour, and a heart that held so much love for the world around him.

Dave, I hope you're looking down on me now, knowing just how dearly privileged I feel to have shared such a special part of your life.

I'll always be proud to come in a close second to the greatest love of your life, your mum.

Rest easy now, Dave.

It's been a long journey home.

But your love will live on in the memories of all who knew you.

Thank you for loving me.

You'll forever be my Dave.

Looking back now, I still wish I'd said more. There was so much that went unspoken.

Since he's passed, those thoughts have lingered in the back of my mind.

And then one night, I had a dream, the kind that stays with you. It left me wondering where dreams come from.

Are they just fragments of memory and emotion that drift through the mind as we sleep?

Or are they something more, a message from another realm, a whisper from someone we've loved, or maybe even a visit?

In the dream, Dave and I stood side by side at the old farm, the sun low on the horizon, its warmth fading, when a carload of critics pulled up, murmuring voices trying to pull him away.

But over it all, I heard him clear and certain: "No," he said. "I'm staying with Brigitte."

As they drove down that familiar limestone driveway, he turned to me and said, "They'll be back. They're gonna turn the volume up on this."

When I woke, the message was crystal clear: I could weather whatever people threw at me. I felt stronger. My hand was already on the dial, ready. Critics might have thought they'd shaken us once, but never again.

In that moment, I knew Dave was still with me, just in a different way now.

Maybe I couldn't share the whole truth in the speech, but I can say it here. Not everything needs a microphone to matter. Sometimes the loudest truths arrive later, in their own time.

And what we can't always put into words, we can carry in music.

So now, I'm turning the volume up, so listen carefully.

Sit back, pour a drink, and put the LP on.

Sing along, and let the music play in your mind.

If you know Dave and me, I'm sure you'll see us in one of these songs. And if you didn't, maybe these songs will remind you of someone you loved.

Our Soundtrack: every song a chapter of our lives, every lyric a memory

1. All Summer Long - Kid Rock

Back when we were all just mates, this song played in the background of our wild youth. Dave and I weren't together yet, but the memories were forming - laughter, drinks, and bonfire nights. You never forget those golden summers.

2. "Chasing Cars" – Snow Patrol

This was our song. From the start, lying up in his sister's spare room, this is what we played. When the world got too loud, too much, "If I lay here, would you lie with me?"

Yes, Dave. Always.

3. "You Shook Me All Night Long" – AC/DC

Rock and roll, plain and simple. Just a nod to sex, drugs, and rock 'n' roll. Dave would've picked this in a heartbeat and would've raised his eyebrows if I didn't include it.

4. "I'll Stand By You" – The Pretenders

Through everything, through all the years - good times and bad, we stood by each other.

5. "Run to Paradise" – The Choirboys

This one reminds me of the years we were still running, still figuring it all out. Sometimes the rules, the obligations, what people thought, it all got too much. We didn't want to follow the rules; we just wanted to run to paradise.

6. "Until I Found You" – Stephen Sanchez

This was Dave's song to me. He played it again and again, and then when the line came, he would sing:

"I would never fall in love again until I found her."

He'd look at me and point, as if to say, That's you. It still makes me cry.

7. "Dancing in the Moonlight" – Toploader

There were moments of feeling alive. Nights lying in the back of the van, watching the moon. We danced in kitchens, at campsites, under stars, still young at heart. This song captures that magic.

8. "Call Me" – Blondie

Dave loved Blondie; she was his hall pass, and he never let me forget it. One day, he asked who mine was, and I shot back, "The postman." Without missing a beat, he came back with,

"What bloody postman? The one who delivers the mail every day?"

That was us, always winding each other up, never too serious. I'd tease him, and he'd fire straight back. I'm sure I even caught him eyeing the postie whenever he went past. And if we weren't together, we were on the phone or yelling out, "Call me," just like the Blondie song he loved

9. "Body Like a Back Road" – Sam Hunt
This song was so Dave. He used to grin and sing,
 "I've got a girl from the Southside."
Then he took off driving like he was in his own film clip. One arm out the window, music up, thinking he was the coolest guy on the road. And maybe he was. He knew every back road around, and he knew me like the back of his hand.

10. "Who Knew" – P!nk
You left me, Dave. You said forever – and I believed you.
"If someone said three years from now, you'd be long gone, I'd stand up and punch them out. 'cause you said forever and ever, who knew?"

Bonus Track: "I'm Still Standing" – Elton John (1983)
Elton John has always been one of my favourites. Ending with, I'm Still Standing feels right. It's about me, still standing, with him in my heart.

The record's finished now, but I can always put it on and play it again. Sometimes it brings an ache to my heart. Other times, I feel a small smile at the corners of my mouth. Our record might not have gone platinum, but to us it was gold.

Chapter 27

My Cup of Tea

Today, of all days, I would give anything to see you walk into the room, in your old pyjamas, with that familiar smile lighting up the space. I can picture it so clearly: your silhouette in the doorway, a steaming cup of tea in hand. I blink, half expecting you to be there, yet it's only a memory now.

How many mornings did we share this simple ritual? That first sip, the warmth spreading through me, softening the edges of the day and preparing me for whatever lay ahead. It was our quiet act of healing. I remember the delicate feel of the china cup in my hands, so familiar and comforting, and the way you would set it down beside me without a word, a small act of love that spoke louder than anything.

Now, a cup of tea holds a different meaning. My dearest ones know how much I adored my collection of teapots and teacups, gifts gathered over the years, but they cannot know the ache that comes with each brew now, the longing for those quiet moments we once shared.

Those cups of tea were our anchor. They gave us a reason to sit side by side. They were there in the sad times, and in the celebrations too. Just a small ritual, one that was ours.

Perhaps one day, I will be remembered as the woman who found solace and connection in something as simple as a cup of tea.

Across cultures, tea carries its own magic: in Japan, the tea ceremony teaches mindfulness and respect; in India, chai welcomes guests and deepens friendships; in Britain, afternoon tea creates cherished moments among friends.

Today, on Valentine's Day, it is everything and yet nothing at all, because I can never share one more cup of tea with you. In life, not everyone is our cup of tea, but you, Dave, were mine. Not only were you the perfect cup of tea, but you were also the warmth that spread through me, brightening every morning. Although I can never share another cup of tea with you, every warm brew echoes the love we once shared, a love that still fills me with warmth.

Chapter 28

The First Anniversary

The celebrations just keep coming: Christmas, Boxing Day, New Year's, Joe's anniversary ...

How much more can one heart bear? To keep facing these days without you.

Today, I lie here with tears rolling down my face. The ache in my chest feels unbearable.

I clutch your old flannel shirt, the one you wore everywhere, even on the hottest days; I feel its worn softness against my skin.

I breathe into your shirt, the one I sleep with. I can't smell you anymore, but the laundry detergent we used in the unit still clings to the fabric. It brings me back to folding your clothes.

Did you say I wash too much?

It's both a comfort and a cruel reminder.

It's the day we chose as our anniversary, 4th February 2010, fifteen years ago, we came together and never looked back. We chose this date to mark something that felt unshakeable, something worth cherishing. Despite our rocky start and years of hiding our feelings, we made it through. And when we were finally free to love each other openly, we still chose to keep this day between us. It was always ours.

If you were here, there wouldn't have been grand plans or over-the-top gestures; that wasn't our way. You would have walked out the front, picked a rose from the bush, and put it in a glass for me, then made me a cup of tea, just like you always did.

We probably would've jumped in the van, taken a slow drive down the South-West Highway, picked up something simple for dinner, your favourite: steak, eggs, and chips, and a treat for later. That would've been enough because we would've been together. And that was always the greatest gift.

But now, there's no one to share this day with. No van, no dinner, no rose in a glass. Only the silence of your absence and the unbearable missing. I'll visit the place where you'll be laid to rest. I'll talk to you like I always do. And I'll remind you, as if you could ever forget, we made it. Against the odds, we made it. And we had a wonderful life.

Even through the heartache, I feel you today.

Not in the way I wish I could, not in the flesh, but in the way love never truly leaves.

I carry you in every beat of this hurting heart.

Happy anniversary, my love.

Chapter 29

It's Not Just a Hanky

Dave was the epitome of old-fashioned charm. He always carried a clean handkerchief, a rarity these days, but to him, it was essential. A hanky is such a small object, yet it tells a big story. In Dave's case, it said everything about his habits and the kind of man he was.

Every time we were heading out, he'd rush back upstairs. I'd hear his laboured breathing as he climbed, then a pause before he called out, "I haven't got a hanky!"

His forgetfulness sometimes frustrated me, but that little ritual never failed to make me smile.

Dave was so accident-prone that his hanky was almost a first-aid kit. A cut finger, a scraped head, a mysterious little bleed from who knows where, out came the hanky to mop it up. It was always there, catching the mess of everyday life.

Whenever I felt sad, Dave would quietly offer his hanky. He'd gently dry my tears and press it into my hands, saying, "Here. It's very crumpled, but it's clean."

Those simple gestures are the ones that linger the most.

During long car rides, my little grandson would call out from the back seat during one of our sing-alongs, "Hang on a minute, Dave!"

I'd laugh and tease, "He needs a hanky, he's got sticky fingers!"

And just like that, one would magically appear.

But the little things don't stay little forever. One day, the handkerchief meant something more.

When the day came for me to say goodbye to Dave, just the two of us, I opened his drawer. Every piece of clothing flashed memories at me: his AC/DC boxer shorts, his socks. All of it felt loud, as if it were saying, "Remember this? Remember me?"

I reached in and found his hanky. How could I not remember him? How could I forget everything we shared?

I came downstairs and plugged in the iron. I ironed that little square perfectly, no creases. Folded it, then folded it again. I cut a small curl of my hair, placed it inside, and sprayed it with his cheap deodorant. I held it as if it were something fragile, as if I were holding him.

Then I made my way to the funeral home, heart pounding, hanky in hand.

When I got to the room, I didn't walk straight over to him. I stood at the door, frightened. I didn't know what he would look like. Would he still look like my Dave?

Slowly, I walked over and there he was.

I touched his spiky hair, his goatee. I gently stroked his cheek, then brushed away an imaginary piece of fluff from his shirt. I tucked the hanky close to his heart. And I could almost hear him say, "You didn't iron that bloody hanky, did you?"

I smiled, leaned forward, and kissed his lips. They were cold. The warmth that once radiated from him was no more. I stood there a moment, just looking at him, memorising him one last time.

He wasn't in pain anymore, and I knew I should have been grateful for that. But at that moment, I was selfish. I wasn't thinking about his peace, I was thinking about mine. I just wanted him here. I wanted the pain in my heart to stop.

I wanted him to hand me a hanky.

I whispered goodbye and I love you over and over as I turned and slowly began to walk from the room. At the door, I quickly turned back. I didn't want to leave him. I kissed him once more.

I knew this was the final goodbye.

Now that Dave is no longer with me, I still carry his hanky. It's dried a million tears over the months. It's not just a hanky, it's so much more.

I still carry one when I visit my grandson, for all the times he needs a handkerchief. I take it with me when I'm nervous or feeling scared and alone. I reach into my pocket and squeeze it, like Dave is giving me strength. It makes me feel close to him.

I'll never look at a hanky without thinking of Dave.

Chapter 30

Grief – Not So Quiet After all

Time passed, like everyone said it would.

Weeks folded into years.

Grief didn't disappear. It sat down beside me and stayed.

During Christmas lunch, amongst all the chatter and laughter, I quietly missed you at the table full of people. I felt very alone.

New Year's, as the sky lit up with fireworks to welcome another year, I thought, *You're not here. My first year, after so many together, without you.*

It doesn't shout like it used to, but it still shows up.

In the garden, when your rosebush blooms.

When I hear one of our songs.

Or when I'm crying or laughing, and I hear your voice saying, "I'm here, my love."

You're just hanging back a little now, encouraging me to try and walk this road alone. But I know you're never far, and somehow, that gives me comfort.

With Joe, grief softened over time, less intense, easier to carry. But losing you, Dave, made it raw again, stirring the ache for Joe too.

It's like a loop I can't quite step out of.

When it gets too much, I let myself feel it.

Some days I curl up on the lounge with our blanket, binge Netflix, eat comfort food, and let the tears fall. It's okay to have those days. I just try not to live there.

I survived that first winter of grief, when the days felt short and the nights endless.

Each morning, I woke to the same grey sky and wondered if the heaviness would ever ease, or if this was simply life now.

Just as it seemed the darkness was lifting, another storm would roll in. It felt impossible to endure.

So, I clung to whatever warmth I could find: a kind word, a memory that made me smile, the comfort of a hand on my shoulder.

And then this morning, when I opened the blinds, a ray of sunshine spilled across my little courtyard. For the first time in a long while, I caught a tiny glimmer of hope.

I had survived the winter – not just metaphorically.

I feel myself slowly growing again, giving it my best shot. Like a little flower pushing up between the cracks in the pavers, tilting towards the sun.

Still, I tread gently, because even in spring, sudden downpours can come without warning.

I'm lucky, I already have love in my life. I love my family, my grandchildren, and my friends.

There are so many forms of love, and my heart has room for all of them.

It still has warmth to give.

Maybe one day I'll meet someone who's loved and lost, too, I could offer companionship and a kind of love, but my heart will always belong to Dave.

I'd need someone who could understand that.

And I can almost hear your voice in my head saying, "Hey, beautiful girl, if you ever want to have coffee with someone, make sure they know how bloody lucky they are. I did. I loved you when you were sad and shattered after Joe, so why wouldn't you be worth loving now? And if someone treats you badly … I swear I'll fucking haunt them."

That was you.

Loyal.

Funny.

Always showing me I was worth loving.

But underneath all of that, no matter what I do, the ache of losing you is always there. I wish it would go away, but it doesn't. Sometimes I wonder how long I'll feel like this, or if this is just my life now. Sadness woven into everything.

Even in the smallest things, it finds me. The other night I had fish and chips for the first time since you've been gone. I sat down on the lounge, unwrapped the paper, and without even thinking, I turned to say, "You want some sauce?" That tiny habit undid me. It reminded me that grief isn't only in the big milestones, it's in the everyday, ordinary moments too.

And yet, even in that ache, I carry a picture in my heart of where I'll meet you again.

I already know what heaven looks like.

There won't be pearly gates, just the old wire gate of the farm.

And when I arrive, you, Dave, will be leaning against the fence, smiling, waiting for me.

We'll embrace, reunited forever.

You'll take my hand and walk me down the driveway, and there'll be Joe, riding his red tractor, raising his arm and calling out, "Hi, love, glad you're home, what's for dinner?"

And just like that, we'll be together again, laughing, loving, with an undeniable energy in another realm, finally all at peace for eternity.

But until that day comes, I'll keep walking.

I'll keep smiling, showing up, taking holidays, and finding small bits of joy with the people who love me.

But deep down, I know I'll never truly recover from losing him. That kind of love leaves a permanent mark.

Chapter 31

The Anger of Grief

Joe is gone now, and most people remember him as a popular, larger-than-life character. I understand that; I feel it too, because there were good parts of him. But it feels different when I carry the weight of his choices. Some days I even find myself shouting into the room, or berating his photograph, "Look what you've bloody done, Joe. Look at the mess you left behind."

I'm angry that he left me to carry the weight of being both parent and grandparent on my own. Angry that I have to justify the choices I've made when so many of his choices made life harder for us while he was alive. And now, because of those choices, he's gone too soon, leaving me with the burden.

When times are tough, when I see the pain in our children's eyes and watch them wrestle with emotions they should never have had to carry, I can't help but feel that anger rise. It's a similar anger I felt with Dave, too. I know he couldn't help getting lung cancer, but I often think he could've looked after himself better. If he hadn't smoked so much, if he hadn't drunk so much, maybe he'd still be here.

Joe left me. He left them. He left us. He left grandchildren who will only ever visit a grave, who will grow up hearing wonderful stories of the myth and the legend. But as they grow, they'll also come to see the saddest truth: that this mythical man is the reason they've watched their mum, their nanny, cry so many tears. In time, they'll understand that love and damage walked hand in hand, and his choices left scars that still reach them today.

And then there's Joe's son. I don't talk about him much, but the truth is, Joe left me to deal with him, too. That's not easy. His self-entitlement, his behaviour, and the way it drains the family still affect us. It used to take all of Joe's physical and emotional energy just to handle him, and now it's me left to shoulder that weight. By the time he's out of jail, I'll be close to seventy, and I honestly don't know if I've got it in me to keep dealing with his whole attitude for the rest of my life.

You should've been here to do that, Joe. You should've been the one to stand between me and all this mess. Instead, I'm left trying to find patience where there is none, while grief keeps hitting me from every angle. Some days, I'm coping; other days, I'm consumed by sadness. There are moments when anger takes over, changing from one hour to the next. Grief doesn't follow a straight path.

Grief has also given me an anger I never had before. Of course, I'd been angry at times, but not like this. This is heavier, sharper. I grieve for the person I once was before it lived inside me, before it kept reshaping who I am. But even with all it has taken, grief can't change my empathy, my compassion, or my love for others.

I had Dave, and even though we could never fix all the broken family dynamics, he made it feel bearable. He'd remind me, "It'll be alright, beautiful girl." That was something. That was hope. Losing him, alongside Joe, has left me in a state of loneliness I've never felt before, where anger and sorrow intertwine.

Still, I know there will be moments throughout my life when I'll miss Joe deeply, when I'll wish he were there for a birthday, a milestone, an ordinary day. And then I feel myself sliding back into the anger of him not being here to share it, just as I feel the weight of Dave's absence looming large, a reminder of what I've lost and what could have been.

Chapter 32

Let's Rock One Last Time

Although grief has changed me, it hasn't taken everything.

At a family breakfast not long ago, just after the new AC/DC tickets went on sale, my two oldest grandkids looked at me and said, "Hey, Nanny, AC/DC tickets are on sale."

I just grinned. "Already got them."

They laughed and fist-pumped. "Yeah, Nanny!"

That's me, in their eyes. Even though they've seen me sad, they still know I'm the Nanny who never misses a good night out.

So, when AC/DC announced their final tour, I didn't even think twice; life's short. I wasn't about to miss it. I wanted to feel alive again – loud, wild, a little reckless, just like the old days.

The minute the tickets went up, my girlfriend and I were online, counting down the seconds and clicking fast. I knew I had to go.

And now it's here.

I've been to every AC/DC concert in Perth, three of them with you and Dave. This one I'll be doing without you. That makes me nervous. But I've got this.

I walk down the stairs in my black mini and AC/DC shirt, trying to channel my inner rock chick. I can almost hear you wolf-whistling from the couch or standing at the bottom of the stairs with your phone out, taking photos and throwing out cheeky lines. You'd lean in, eyebrow raised, and say, "Wanna pick me up?" hoping I'd say yes. And I probably would.

It's the Power Up tour. The end of an era. For AC/DC. For you. And, in a way, for me too.

The date stings: 4th December. Just two days after the first anniversary of your passing. It only seems fitting, though. You'd be buzzing, unable to contain your excitement, and I can see it all so clearly.

Living easy, loving free. That was us.

So tonight, just for you, I'm going to be young again. Even though I'm (mostly) responsible these days, I'll do exactly what you would've told me: let's get shitfaced.

I'll wear my AC/DC shirt as proudly as you wore yours every single day of your life. I'll throw my hands in the air with your rock-on signal, thumb and pinkie out, the rest clenched tight, and I'll do it for you.

And when the stage lights blaze and the crowd roars, I'll let the music take me back to us, back to those nights when love and rock 'n' roll was all we needed.

So tonight, I'll rock out for both of us. I'll feel you in every song, every beat, and in my heart, always.

Chapter 33

Final Word

After many tears and just as many smiles, my story comes to an end.

Well ... this chapter, anyway.

After half a century, I can finally breathe again.

Telling my story has done that.

It has brought me profound peace.

Whatever you take from it, I just hope you judge it kindly.

Life isn't black and white. We all do our best with what we've been given.

I'm not ashamed of the life I've lived.

Above all, I'm proud.

Proud that I survived.

That I kept showing up.

And loved, even when it was hard.

We were good people, despite our flaws.

I'm kind, too kind at times, and I always try to see the good in others.

Dave didn't have much, yet he always gave to those in need.

I once saw him give his only jumper to a cold man. That was just who he was. His hand was always there to hold, especially when I needed it most.

Joe, if he loved you, you knew it.

And if he didn't, you knew that too.

He wasn't perfect, but he had love and undeniable strength.

He made me laugh, but also frustrated me deeply.

We had real happiness, even if it didn't last in the way we once hoped.

I sometimes feel guilty for my happiness with Dave. I always loved Joe, but things got complicated. Life got harder. I loved him differently by then, but it was still love. Finding deep happiness with Dave didn't erase my love for Joe; it was simply different, and there was room in my heart for both of them.

My children are good people, despite their beginnings. They are solid and kind.

They're thoughtful parents who care about others in ways that matter.

I'm proud of who they've become.

We made mistakes.

We endured addiction, heartbreak, grief, and mess.

But we also laughed.

We built families.

We loved each other with everything we had.

The people we hurt the most were usually ourselves.

Writing this memoir helped me realise something I didn't expect:

For a long time, that little girl who didn't know where she belonged kept searching.

I thought my place had to be out there, in people, towns, relationships.

It took decades, and plenty of heartbreak, to realise I already carried it inside me.

Dave helped me see that I didn't have to keep searching. The place I was looking for was already in me. And with him beside me, I finally believed I was enough.

The boys don't want me to be superhuman. They just want me to live, to be happy.

It's strange reaching the end of this story. A bit scary, too. But I know this much: I've made it through a lot, and I'll keep going.

And if you're still searching for your place, like I once was, remember, you're not alone.

So next time you watch the sun rise or set, take a moment to be thankful
- for love, in all its forms.
- for the people who've been, those who stay, and those yet to come.

Let love in.

If you're lucky enough to have a hand to hold – a family member's, a friend's, or the love of your life – hold onto that love.

It's a beautiful gift.

Love always,

Brigitte xx

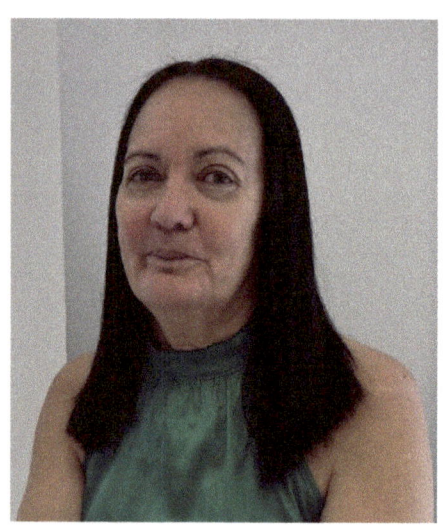

About the Author

Hidden in Plain Sight is Brigitte's first book, though she has spent a lifetime journaling and capturing memories in words. She raised her family and built her career in Kwinana, where her roots run deep.

Now living in Rockingham, Brigitte spends her days in her garden, a place of reflection and peace, surrounded by her children, grandchildren, and dearest friends. Writing has become her way of honouring the past, and now she looks forward to the future, perhaps even dusting off her children's book manuscripts and seeing where the words take her next.

www.ingramcontent.com/pod-product-compliance
Lightning Source LLC
Chambersburg PA
CBHW040107100526
44584CB00029BA/3862